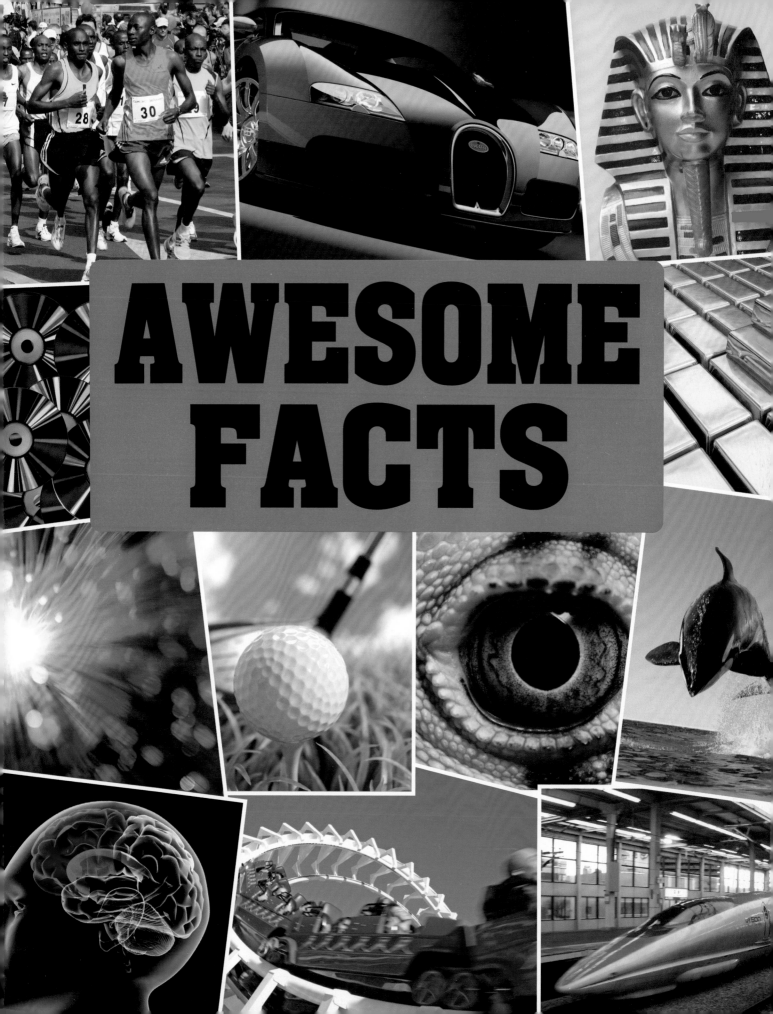

AWESOME FACTS

AWESOME FACTS

igloo

igloo

New edition published in 2010
by Igloo Books Ltd
Cottage Farm
Sywell
NN6 0BJ

www.igloo-books.com

Designed by Essential Works

10 9 8 7 6 5 4 3

ISBN: 978-1-84817-765-9

Printed and manufactured in China

Contents

Introduction

Who is the greatest swimmer of modern times? Which region of the Earth had no rain for 400 years? When were the first commercial CDs pressed? And more importantly, where in the world can you go to find out all of this and much, much more? The answer is – right here!

Welcome to *Awesome Facts*, the greatest book of the biggest, the best, the oldest, the richest, the fastest, the tallest, the youngest, the deepest, the furthest, and the longest.

In this book we cover extraordinary categories such as dragons and mythical beasts, the paranormal, the world's most unusual buildings, forensics, robots, creatures of the deep – even the human face! The wildest and the wackiest on soccer, dinosaurs, computers, marathons, discoveries, mountains, reptiles, music, civilizations and movies is combined with the straightforward. Platform shoes, a tree that's almost 5,000 years old, the movie franchise that's bigger than Bond, the world's smelliest town, the most haunted house, the age of the oldest turtle – they're all here – fascinating facts and figures that entertain as much as they inform.

There are traditional records and facts on board games, the world around us, feats

of strength, athletics, and cartoons. But because technology and trends never sit still, *Awesome Facts* is also up to the minute, with new records and facts on categories including the X Games, computer games, extreme sports and CGI SFX in the movies. As you look through, you'll find out records on base jumping, discover which computer game is the most eagerly-awaited, which is the movie with the most expensive SFX and who is the best snowboarder in the world.

This book also includes the detail behind the record, so you can find out about the vulture whose skin changes color; that crocodiles cry after they've eaten a meal; that feathers from a goose's left wing make better badminton shuttlecocks than feathers from a goose's right wing. Did you know that the Chinese were using technology similar to Gutenberg's writing press centuries before he invented it, or that the Internet was originally called the Intergalactic Computer Network? If you read on, you will find out much more. Just get going!

Our Amazing Planet

There are world records being broken in all manner of topics so, to make it as easy as possible for you to find your way around *Awesome Facts*, we have split this book into eight different sections. Each category is as exciting and as fascinating as the next, so the only problem you'll have is deciding where to start.

The HUMAN BODY section looks at how our bodies work and to what extremes we can go. Along with the tallest, the oldest, and the hairiest, you'll find out how babies learn, why our faces are special, and what we do when we get together in large groups. In SPORTS, you'll be able to look up some of the strangest sporting records – lunar golf, for example, and the most coconuts smashed with punches. You can access any sport you can think of, from base jumping and skateboarding, to NBA basketball and soccer.

SCIENCE & TECHNOLOGY covers the humble beginnings of many things we take for granted – the telephone, the television, the Internet – and brings you up to date on the biggest, best, and most expensive-to-develop computer games. On a completely different level, the ANIMAL KINGDOM and PLANET EARTH look at the wonders of the natural world and things that have not changed for thousands of years. The fastest, the oldest, the most dangerous are all here, as are the great volcanoes, rivers, oceans, and trees – and don't forget the dinosaurs.

The world of celebrities and their achievements can be found in ARTS & ENTERTAINMENT, which also covers record-breaking music, books and movies – the most expensive movies do not necessarily prove to be the most popular. HUMAN ACHIEVEMENT examines what people have accomplished through the ages, from the intrepid explorers and mountaineers to space travel and bridge-building, and from the wildest stunts to the works of the great humanitarians.

Finally, PEOPLE & PLACES looks at what makes each person around the planet unique, and how the environments we exist in have helped to shape us. Did you know the Japanese have a different counting system from the rest of the world? And that dozens of new words are added to the English language every year?

First sub-10 sec 100 meters

This was considered another "impossible" achievement, but Jim Hines' record time of 9.9sec that he set on 20 June 1968 in California, USA, stood for 15 years. The women's world record has stood at 10.49sec since 1988, achieved by Florence Griffith-Joyner.

The Grand Slam of tennis

In tennis, winning the French Open, Wimbledon, US Open, and the Australian Open in the same calendar year amounts to completing the "Grand Slam". The first man to do it was Don Budge, in

sweep of golf's big four prizes – the US Open, the British Open, the US Amateur, and the British Amateur – in 1930. It has never been done since, and, in the modern Grand Slam, the two amateur championships have been replaced with the Masters and the PGA.

Soccer league champions & FA Cup double

In the 1888/89 season, Preston North End, UK, was the first team to win the League and the FA Cup in the same year. Back then, the First Division (the equivalent of the current Premiership) only had 12 teams, and Tottenham Hotspur won the first Double of modern soccer in the 1960/61 season. Since then, Arsenal have won it three times (1970/71, 1997/98, 2001/2), Manchester United three times (1993/94, 1995/96, 1998/99), and Liverpool once (1985/86).

The first 4-minute mile

Roger Bannister was the first person to run the mile in under four minutes, running 3min 59.4sec on 6 May 1954 at the Iffley Road racetrack in Oxford, UK. At the time, this was believed to be impossible, as the previous record of 4min 1.4sec had stood for nine years. Today, the record is 3min 43.13sec, and under four minutes is a starting point for serious middle-distance runners. No female athlete has yet run the mile in under four minutes; however, it will probably happen soon, as the current world record is 4min 12.56sec, set by Sveltlana Masterkova of Russia in 1996.

1938, and the first woman was Maureen Connolly in 1953 – both from California. Since then, only Rod Laver (1962 and 1969), Margaret Court (1970), and Steffi Graf (1988) have achieved this feat.

Golf's Grand Slam

The American Bobby Jones made a clean

F1 Grand Prix

The first F1 race took place on 1 September 1946 in Turin, Italy, and was won by Archille Varzi. The "formula" is a set of rules which every participant and car must meet. The formula was originally based on pre-war regulations defined by engine capacity.

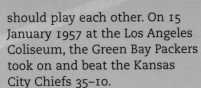

Original superbowl

This spectacular finale to the gridiron season, the American football season, was arranged after the National Football League (NFL) and the American Football League (AFL) joined forces in 1966 and decided each division's champions should play each other. On 15 January 1957 at the Los Angeles Coliseum, the Green Bay Packers took on and beat the Kansas City Chiefs 35–10.

A special cricket Test Match

The first cricket test match commenced on 15 March 1877, between England and Australia at Melbourne Cricket Ground, Australia. The official definition of a Test Match at that time was "a test of strength and competency" between the two sides. At the March 1877 match, Australia proved to be the stronger and more competent side, winning by 45 runs.

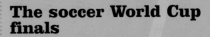

The soccer World Cup finals

When it was announced that soccer would not be included in the 1932 Olympic Games in Los Angeles, due to the low popularity of the game in the US, FIFA President Jules Rimet planned the inaugural soccer World Cup tournament, to be held in Uruguay in 1930. The original trophy was named after him. 13 countries took part, and the cup was won by the hosts, who beat Argentina 4–2 before a crowd of 93,000 in the capital Montevideo.

The smallest giraffe

The okapi is very rare and can only be found in the forests of central Africa, where it was discovered 100 years ago. First thought to be a type of horse, the okapi is now known as the "forest giraffe," as it is the only known species related to the giraffe. It's much smaller, though. While the giraffe grows up to 18ft (5.5m) tall, the okapi rarely grows higher than about 5.5ft (1.7m).

The rodent as big as a pig

The capybara, a huge semi-aquatic rodent which only lives in South America, is the world's largest rodent, measuring up to 4ft 3in (1.3m) long. Its name means "master of the grasses" and it eats up to 8lb (3.6kg) of grass and aquatic plants every day.

The sleepiest squirrel in the US

The Uinta ground squirrel is quite common in the mountain meadows of western USA but you'll have to pick the right time to spot it, because it is the sleepiest mammal. It becomes dormant in July because of the heat and then hibernates underground during the cold of autumn and winter. However, it does have one very special skill: each year it tells us when Spring has truly arrived, because only then does it come out from its hiding place.

The hedgehog that lays eggs

Apart from the duck-billed platypus, the echidna is the only mammal that lays eggs, which it then hatches in a warm pouch like that of a kangaroo. Very prickly, with a long snout, the echidna resembles hedgehogs and porcupines. It lives in New Guinea and Australia and is named after a half-human monster in Greek mythology.

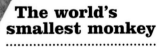

The rare vulture whose skin changes color

The Californian condor is a North American vulture and is the rarest bird of prey. It's a real record-breaker because, with a wingspan of 9ft (2.7m), it is the biggest bird in North America and it can live to be 50 years old. Its skin changes color from yellow to bright red depending on what sort of mood it is in. The US's most expensive species conservation project has helped to stop it becoming extinct.

Miniature Asian deer

One of the world's smallest deer is the leaf deer, which was not discovered until 1997 in the jungle of Southeast Asia. Also known as the leaf muntjac, the adults are only about 2ft (60cm) tall and the males' antlers are about 1.5in (3.8cm) long.

The most useful nose

The pig-like tapir has a big rear-end and its face has a prehensile snout, which means that, like an elephant, it can use its nose to grab things and can point it in different directions for a better sense of smell. There are four different types of tapirs in Asia, Central America, and South America, but unfortunately they are all becoming endangered. They are the final survivors of a family of mammals that have not changed for 20 million years.

The world's smallest monkey

The tiniest of all types of monkey, the pygmy marmoset's body is about the size of an adult hand (5.5in/14cm). They are so light that, unlike most animals, they can eat the highest leaves on the weakest branches of a tree, but they spend most of their time gouging tree bark, looking for the sap, which is their favorite food.

on top of Mount Graham, which is a 10,700ft (3,261m) mountain in south eastern Arizona, USA. The first light images for the LBT were captured in January 2008, and show the galaxy NGC 2770, which is located 88 million light-years from the Milky Way.

Life on Earth

Our solar system, which revolves around the sun, consists of eight planets which, from the sun, are Mercury, Venus, Earth, Mars, Jupiter, Saturn, Uranus, and Neptune. The Earth is approximately 93 million miles (150 million km) from the Sun, and is the only planet in the Solar System, as far as we know, to support life.

Most powerful telescope

The Large Binocular Telescope (LBT) is the most powerful ever built and is actually two 27ft (8.4m) telescopes placed side-by-side. Although they're separate, they work together to act like a single, much larger telescope. The $120 million (£80 million) LBT is located

28,000
light years between youngest star and Earth

Space beyond the Milky Way

Edwin Hubble (1889–1953), an American astronomer, was the first person to prove that we live in an expanding universe. Hubble discovered that ours is not the only galaxy to exist – there are others out there beyond the Milky Way.

How old is planet Earth?

Bishop Ussher is believed to have made the earliest recorded attempt to calculate the age of the Earth. He did this by following the family trees as described in the Bible. In the 17th century the Bishop estimated that the Earth and the Universe was created in October 4004BCE. Physicist Claire Patterson, however, made an alternative estimate in 1965. She calculated that the Earth was 4,560 million years old.

The first recognized comet

Edmond Halley was the first astronomer to discover that comets have periodic orbits. In 1705, he accurately predicted that the comet now known as Halley's comet would return in 1758. It takes Halley's comet 76 years to complete its orbit and there are records of every return of this particular comet since 240BCE.

Crash, bang, wallop

Most meteorites burn up before they hit the Earth, so are usually harmless to humans. The earliest, and only, recorded instance of anybody being hit by one was in the USA in 1954, when a space rock the size of a cricket ball crashed through Ann Hodges' roof and struck her on the arm.

The youngest star in the galaxy

In May 2008, astronomers using NASA's Chandra X-ray Observatory and the Very Large Array radio telescope in New Mexico made a breakthrough discovery. They found the remains of a supernova, known as "G1.9", which must have lit up our galaxy with a bright flash of light about 140 years ago. That makes the "G1.9" the youngest known supernova in the Milky Way. The supernova's remains are estimated to be situated approximately 28,000 light years away, close to the center of the Milky Way.

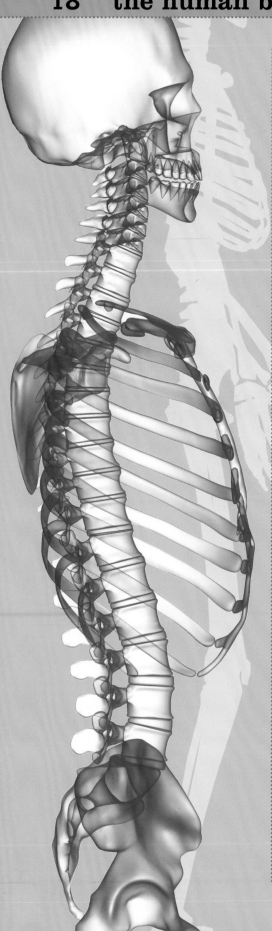

The world's largest feet

Matthew McGrory did have the world's largest feet even though he wasn't the world's tallest man: he was only 7ft 6in (2.27m) tall. Born in Pennsylvania, McGrory earned his place in the history books with size 29 US shoes, which is around 18in (45cm) long. He also found fame after being cast in Tim Burton's fantasy film *Big Fish*, as Karl the Giant. He died of natural causes aged 32 in 2005.

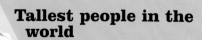

World's longest beard

An average beard grows 5.5in (14cm) in a year and, in an average lifespan, men trim off 7.7lb (3.5kg) of whisker hair. Knowing that, Hans Langseth of Norway's beard was an incredible achievement. When he died in 1927, his beard measured 17.5ft (533cm) – it's now an exhibit at the Smithsonian Institute in Washington DC, USA.

Tallest people in the world

Sultan Kösen of Turkey, the tallest man at 8ft 1in (2.46m), also has the world's largest hands, 10.8in (27.5cm), and feet – 14.4in (36.5cm). Yao Defen of China is the world's tallest woman at 7ft 8in (2.37m), and earns a living as an itinerant performer. In both cases, growth has been caused by the pituitary gland releasing excess growth hormone due to a tumor. Robert Pershing Wadlow, the tallest person of all time, was 8ft 11.1in (2.47m), and still growing, at the time of his death at 22.

Longest fingernails

Lee Redmond of Salt Lake City, Utah, continues to hold the record for the world's longest fingernails at 28ft 3.7in (8m 65cm) when last measured in February 2008. However, her nails broke in February 2009 when she was

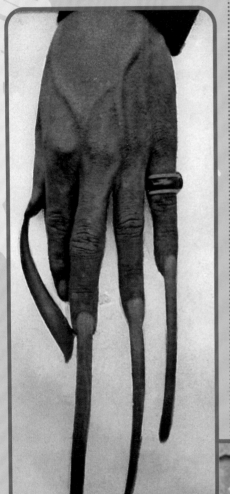

Heaviest people in the world

With his peak weight reaching 1400lb (635kg), John Brower Minnoch has been the heaviest man to date. After 16 months on a strict diet, he weighed 476lb (216kg), his shedding of 924lb (419kg) being the largest documented weight loss. He died in 1983. Robert Earl Hughes, who died in 1958, held the record in his lifetime, weighing 1,070lb (486kg). However, the record for the world's heaviest person rests with Carol Yager who was estimated to weigh 1600lb (726kg) at her peak, and died in 1994 weighing 1200lb (544kg). She was able to neither stand nor walk.

Oldest person

The oldest person in the world was Jeanne Calment from Provence in France. She was born in 1875 and died in 1997 aged 122 years and 164 days. In second place, Shigechiyo Izumi from Japan is said to be the world's oldest man. Allegedly born in 1865, he died on 21 February in 1986 aged 120 years and 237 days.

Longest moustache

Badamsinh Juwansinh Gurjar from Ahmedabad, India, holds the record for the world's longest moustache, at 12.5ft (3.81m). He had not cut his relatively unstylish moustache for 22 years, in order to achieve this record. Despite his moustache's length, his hair isn't the most valuable in the world. That honor goes to Lord Nelson of England. A lock of his hair was sold at auction for $11,017 (£7,200), on 18 February 1988 by a bookseller from Cirencester, UK.

ejected from a car in an accident. She had been growing her nails since late-1978.

Urban legends

In 1986 hip-hop legends Run DMC's album *Raising Hell* became the first platinum-selling rap album. Their collaboration with Aerosmith on the single "Walk this Way" saw hip-hop break in to the pop charts for the first time. In 1988, DJ Jazzy Jeff & the Fresh Prince won the first Grammy for rap music, and in 1989 Tone Loc's "Wild Thing" became hip-hop's first certified platinum single.

Show me the money

The highest amount ever paid for a musical instrument at a public auction is $2.03 million (£1.3m). Christie's auctioneers in New York sold the "Lady Tennant" violin in 2005. In 1998, Christie's auctioned a similar Stradivarius violin, made one year earlier than the Lady

Old-time rockers

EMI Group PLC is the oldest record company in the world, dating back to 1897. The company owns many famous labels known throughout the world such as Parlophone, Virgin Records, Blue Note jazz label, and dance label Positiva.

$450,000
record price paid for a guitar

Tennant, for $880,000 (£577,280). Collecting and buying violins is clearly a good investment as the value of famous old violins more than doubled in seven years.

I will always love you

The best-selling movie soundtrack album is *The Bodyguard: Official Soundtrack Album*. It features six songs by Whitney Houston and songs from other famous artists of the time. The album sold over 17 million copies in the US, and 42 million copies worldwide. The movie starred Houston alongside Kevin Costner.

Singing for his dinner

When the great former Italian tenor Luciano Pavarotti combined his love of soccer and music to sing Puccini's aria "Nessun dorma" at the 1990 World Cup finals, he became the first opera singer to perform a World Cup tournament anthem. Following that, his concerts were as big as his girth, and in 1993 he set a record for concert attendance in London, when 150,000 turned up to see him in Hyde Park. Later that year he performed for 500,000 in New York's Central Park, and in 1994 sang for 300,000 people under the Eiffel Tower in Paris.

The beginning of the video star

American cable television network MTV (Music Television) was launched on 1 August 1981. Based in New York City, in the US MTV was the first successful channel whose purpose was to play music videos in their entirety. MTV has revolutionized the music industry. The first music video shown on MTV was "Video Killed the Radio Star" by The Buggles. The second video shown was Pat Benatar's "You Better Run". The first video to be rejected by MTV was "Girls on Film" by Duran Duran. The same year that it was launched the station would not play the video because it contained full-frontal nudity. It was later cut so that it could be aired.

Just a country girl

Country singer LeAnn Rimes was only 14-year-old when she won a Grammy (US music industry award) in the "best new artist" category at the 1997 Grammy awards. This was the first time a country singer had won the award, and she was also the youngest singer of country music to win any Grammy.

Seal of approval

The first stamp issued in the US in 2007 had the face of Ella Fitzgerald on it. She became the 30th person to be honored by the Black Heritage Commemorative Stamp Series. The first musician to be honored in such a way was composer and musician Scott Joplin in 1983.

Youngest drivers on the F1 circuit

Jaime Alguesuari of Spain is the youngest driver to have competed in a Formula One race. He was 19 years 125 days old when he drove in the Hungarian Grand Prix in 2009, beating Canadian Mike Thackwell's 1980 record of 19 years 182 days.

Youngest F1 winners

The youngest Formula one winner is Sebastian Vettel of Germany, who won the Italian Grand Prix in 2008 aged just 21 years and 73 days.

Driving Mr Chinon

The oldest driver ever to compete in a Formula One race was Frenchman Louis Chinon. When he took on the rest in the 1955 Monaco Grand Prix, Chinon was 55 years 292 days' old. He finished sixth.

Round, round, baby

NASCAR stands for the National Association for Stock Car Auto Racing, and is by far the biggest motor sport in the United States. In terms of popularity NASCAR ranks above NBA basketball and is second only to NFL soccer. NASCAR races take place on oval tracks that are between one and four miles (1.6 and 6.4km) per circuit, races are 400 or 500 miles (643 or 805km) long – which is a lot of laps! – and the cars always go round the track anticlockwise.

Fasten your seatbelts

The fastest woman drag racer is Melanie Troxel, who reached an incredible 330.3mph (530kph) in 2005; the fastest man is Tony Schumacher (no relation to the rather more famous Michael), who clocked 337.58mph (533kph) in the same year.

It pays to race

Jeff Gordon is NASCAR's most successful driver, having won 82 races and five championships since 1992. Gordon has racked up total career earnings of "$102,977,287 (£67,553,100), winning over $23,400,000 (£15,090,000) in 2009 alone.

Schumi, he's the best

Michael Schumacher, of Germany, has the most Formula One wins under his belt, with 91 from 250 races between 1991 and 2006, giving him an incredible success rate of 36.4 per cent. In 2010, Schumacher came out of retirement to join Mercedes GP for a season back in Formula One following a three-year absence.

NASCAR record

The highest number of cars to start a NASCAR race was 36, in the 2006 Allstate 400.

Keeping it in the family

Richard Petty is considered the greatest NASCAR driver of all time, winning 200 races in an amazingly successful career that lasted from 1958 to 1984, including seven Daytona 500s and winning the NASCAR Drivers' Championship a record seven times. His father Lee was a NASCAR champion too and his son Kyle is currently driving, hoping to get into the record books.

Short and sweet, and very quick

The NRHA is the America's National Hot Rod Association, which oversees most drag racing events. Drag racing sets two cars against each other over a quarter mile (402m) straight track from a standing start. Drag race cars burning "top fuel", a mixture of nitromethane and petrol, can achieve speeds of over 300mph (500kph) with acceleration faster than the Space Shuttle.

The P34 didn't reign in Spain

The only six-wheeled car ever to race at Formula One level was the Tyrell P34. It was thought that the P34 would reduce drag because it had two sets of small wheels at the front and one normal-sized set at the rear. It first ran in the Spanish Grand Prix in 1976, and started a further 29 races, winning just once in Sweden in that same year.

Ocean front

The oceans contain enough salt to cover all the continents to a depth of nearly 500ft (152m) and an estimated 80% of all life on earth is found under the ocean surface. The oceans contain 99% of the living space on the planet. At least 70% of the world is covered by water – mainly salt-water oceans. The oceans are also divided into four major basins: the Pacific, Atlantic, Indian, and Arctic Oceans, and they're interconnected with various shallow seas, such as the Mediterranean Sea, the Gulf of Mexico, and the South China Sea. The remaining 30% of the Earth's surface consists of mountains, deserts, plains, plateaus, and other geomorphologies.

Secret icebergs

During World War II, there was a secret program known as Habbakuk in operation, which planned to manufacture icebergs for use as aircraft carriers.

Deepest place

The deepest place on Earth is the Challenger Deep in the Mariana Trench, off Guam in the Pacific Ocean. The trench is 35,899ft (10,924m) below sea level – that's at least a mile (1.6km) deeper than Mt Everest is high.

Melting pot

If Antarctica's 6,000,000 cu miles of ice melted, then all the level of the oceans all over the world would rise at least 200ft (61m).

Fastest current

The Kuroshio Current, off the shores of Japan, is the World's fastest current. It can travel between 25–75mp/day (40–121km /day) at 1–3mph (1.6–4.8kph), and is 3,301ft (1,006m) deep.

High tides

The highest tides in the world are at the Bay of Fundy, which separates New Brunswick from Nova Scotia. Almost every day, twice a day, the bay empties and fills with 100 billion tonnes of water, creating a difference between high and low tide of 53ft (16.3m).

The world's longest river

There is a huge debate about which river holds the title of "world's longest". Some scientists argue that it's the Nile, while others say it's the Amazon. The length of the river is hard to calculate, as scientists can't always identify the source and mouth. Recent reports from researchers in Brazil claim that the Amazon measures 4,250 miles (6,800km) compared to the Nile's 4,160 miles (6,695km). However, the Amazon carries the greater volume of water: every day 500 billion cu ft (14 million cu meters) flow into the Atlantic.

The world's deepest freshwater lake

One of the coldest places on Earth, Siberia in Russia, is home to the world's deepest lake. Lake Baikal is a natural freshwater lake that has been measured at 5,712ft (1,741m) deep – more than a mile.

Capped ice

Nearly 90 per cent of the Earth's ice covers either Greenland or Antarctica, home to ice caps and ice sheets. Ice sheets cover an area over 19,305 sq miles (50,000 sq km) while ice caps cover areas smaller than that. The Earth's polar ice caps are mainly water ice, while the polar ice caps on Mars are a mixture of carbon dioxide and water ice.

Largest ocean

The Pacific ocean is the world's largest water body and it occupies a third of the Earth's surface. The Pacific contains about 25,000 islands (more than the total number in the rest of the world's oceans combined), almost all of which are found south of the equator. The Pacific covers an area of 69.4 million sq miles (179.7 million sq km).

Niagara Falls

The most famous falls in the world are Niagara Falls. The Canadian "Horseshow" half of Niagara Falls are 180ft (60m) high and are 2,500ft (833m) wide. The depth of Niagara River just below the "Horseshow" is also 180ft (60m), which is as deep as the Niagara Gorge walls are high. Niagara Falls is the second largest falls in the world after Victoria Falls on the Zambezi river in southern Africa. The world's highest falls are Angel Falls in Venezuela, South America, which are 979m (3212ft) high.

The saltiest sea

The Dead Sea is 8.9 times saltier than the average ocean: 31.5 per cent of the Deep Sea is salt, as compared to 3.5 per cent of the Mediterranean. It is 1,378ft (420m) below sea level and its shores are the lowest point on the surface of the Earth, on dry ground. It is 1,083ft (330m) deep, the deepest hypersaline lake in the world.

The Everglades

The Everglades is the sweetest place in America – there are roughly 664 sq miles (1,720 sq km) of sugar cane in the southern US and more than half of those acres are in the Everglades in Florida. The Everglades themselves are made up of 10,000 different islands, and the Everglades National Park consists of 2,185 sq miles (6,569 sq km).

Coral sea

The Red Sea, which runs between Africa and Arabia, is the only enclosed Coral Sea and is the world's most northern tropical sea.

Fresh lakes

Filled with six quadrillion gallons of fresh water, the Great Lakes contain one-fifth of the world's fresh surface water. Only the polar ice caps and Lake Baikal in Siberia, Russia, contain more water.

Saved by mould!

The greatest discovery in medicine, saving millions of lives, happened in 1928. A Scottish scientist called Alexander Fleming (1881–1955) realized that a mould called penicillium stopped the growth of bacteria. The mould was used to make penicillin, an antibiotic, which kills bacteria that cause life-threatening infections and diseases.

The gravity apple

In 1666, the British physicist Sir Isaac Newton (1643–1727) discovered gravity. He was quietly thinking when he witnessed an apple fall from a tree and

The most famous discovery moment

Archimedes (287–212BCE), the Ancient Greek thinker, was getting in the bath when he suddenly shouted "Eureka!", which means "I have found it". He ran out in the streets naked, shouting and waving

consequently worked out three laws explaining the force of gravity on objects. These laws became the foundations of classical mechanics.

Theory of relativity

Albert Einstein (1879–1955) is considered to be one of the brainiest people ever. In 1915, the German scientist was the first person to work out that gravity is a

1492
year Columbus discovered the Americas

his arms around. He was so excited because he had just realized that if you float an object in water, the water will rise according to the weight of the object. This principle of buoyancy has been used ever since to help boats to float. The term "Eureka moment" is used whenever someone has a sudden realization.

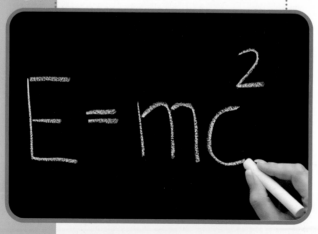

property of the geometry of space and time. This means that space, time, and objects act differently in different circumstances because they are relative to each other. This general theory of relativity allows scientists to understand many things about the cosmos, light, and time. It's very complicated, though! Luckily, Einstein himself had a brain that was considerably larger than that of an average human.

The New World

The European explorer Christopher Columbus (1451–1506) is said to have been the first person to discover the Americas in 1492. However, the Vikings landed in Canada as early as the 11th century, and it is possible that Polynesians from the Pacific Ocean had contact with South America centuries before then. In fact, America was first "discovered" by the indigenous people who had been living there for at least 20,000 years!

Galvani understood that electricity runs through our system to make our muscles move. This led to the invention of the battery. The word "galvanize," which means "to spur into action," is named after him.

Vital vitamins

In 1929 Sir Frederick Hopkins (1861–1947) and Christiaan Eijkman (1858–1930) were awarded the Nobel Prize for being the first to establish a link between vitamins and good health. A lack of vitamins in the diet can cause illness and even death.

Navigation by stars

In 1837, US sea captain Thomas Hubbard Sumner (1807–76) became the first person to discover how to use the stars to plot both longitude and latitude at the same time. Sailors have always used the sun, moon, and stars to help them navigate the seas but this new system gave a skipper the exact position of a boat. The system was the forerunner of the Global Positioning System (GPS), which uses satellites instead of stars.

Get galvanized!

Italian biologist Luigi Galvani (1737–98) discovered that humans contain electricity. He was dissecting a dead frog one day when his assistant touched a nerve with a scalpel that had been exposed to static electricity. The frog's leg kicked as if it was alive. As a result,

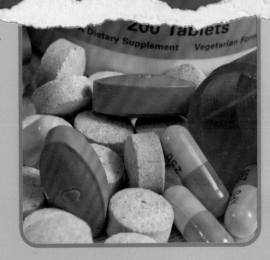

The best inventors

The Ancient Chinese were the best inventors in the world. Many modern-day things were invented by them hundreds of years before they were used in the West. They were also very interested in philosophy and medicine. The Chinese were the first people to develop printing, use paper money, invent explosives, and create porcelain (which is sometimes called "china"). They even invented noodles 4,000 years ago!

The greatest ancient civilization

Whilst most other races were still trying to make fire, the Ancient Egyptians (3000–30BCE) erected buildings that would last for thousands of years, created the first large irrigation system for farming, and established the most advanced written language, mathematic, and legal systems. The pyramids are the oldest large buildings that are still standing.

The first explorers

The Phoenicians (1200–332BCE) of the Middle East were seafarers who were the greatest explorers until the Vikings over 1,000 years later. They were interested in trade. They circumnavigated the whole of Africa and travelled throughout the Mediterranean, setting up cities. The Phoenicians also spread the use of their alphabet, which is the basis for modern-day alphabets.

The great road builders

The Incas created the largest empire (AD1200–1532) in the Americas. It ran the length of South America. To make travel easy, they built an amazing system of roads that was more advanced than anywhere else in the world. They were very precise stonemasons, building long-lasting structures. Machu Picchu in Peru is one of the world's greatest historical sites. However, the Incas didn't learn to use the wheel or how to write.

The early Indians

The great ancient Indian culture was the Indus Valley civilization of Harappa and Mohenjo-daro. These large cities flourished in 2500 to 1700BCE. They had what may have been the first written language, lived in brick houses, and had domesticated animals.

These cities even had what is thought to be the first sanitation system. The ancient cities were not discovered until the 1920s.

The most advanced Central Americans

The Aztecs were the most advanced civilization in Central America. They did many things that had never been achieved before. They reclaimed marshland to build their huge capital city, Tenochtitlán, and created their own empire (AD1200–1524).

Astronomers and mathematicians

The ancient Maya of Central America were fantastic astronomers, accurately charting the movement of the planets. In order to do their calculations they started to use the number zero by about 30BCE. Europeans didn't work out how useful the zero could be until over a millennium later! They also had an advanced written language.

The original New Zealanders

The first New Zealanders were not the Europeans that landed there after Captain Cook found the islands in the 18th century. The Maoris, which means "the originals," had come from Polynesia at least 500 years earlier to settle on the land. European colonization and diseases almost wiped them out. Now the Maoris make up 15 per cent of the New Zealand population. The national rugby team uses the haka, the fierce Maori dance, to intimidate rivals before matches.

The longest day

The longest tennis rally to be acknowledged by the US Tennis Association lasted 9h 7min, and consisted of 17,062 shots. The rally was during a match played between Rob Peterson and Ray Miller in San Diego, California, in February 2000.

Speeding shuttle

Badminton is the fastest racket sport, with the record for shuttlecock speed standing at 206mph (332kph), set by Fu Haifeng of China, in June 2005.

Mind-boggling global figures

The first Wimbledon final in 1877 was watched by just 200 people, but in 2007, thanks to television, the men's final had an audience of over 2 billion.

33
age of the oldest tennis number one

Team China

Table tennis became an Olympic sport in 1988; since then it has been dominated by the Chinese, who have won 20 table tennis golds in total.

Best shuttlecocks

The world's finest shuttlecocks, made by hand, have 16 feathers from the left wing of a goose.

Best badminton players

China and Indonesia have won over 75 per cent of all International Badminton Federation events between them.

The world's most popular racquet sport

This is table tennis, with over 10 million players competing in organized competitions every year.

The longest recorded tennis match

It took Pancho Gonzales, from USA, 5h 12min to beat Charles Pasarell, from -San Juan, Puerto Rico, in 112 games in 1969. The longest rally was 643 shots, between Vicki Nelson-Dunbar and Jean Hepner, both from the USA, in Virginia, USA, in 1984. The match itself took over six hours and included a 1h 47min tie-break, during which one point took half an hour.

Most intriguing ban

Table tennis was banned in the Soviet Union from 1930 to 1950 because it was believed to be harmful to the eyes – but nobody ever quite worked out why!

Ping pong facts

The fastest rally was 173 shots in 60 sec, between the American Jackie Bellinger and Lisa Lomas of England, in London, in 1993. The longest rally was 18h 15min 1sec, between Brian and Steven Seibel of the USA in Arizona, in 2004.

Fastest serve

Men: 155mph (249kph); Andy Roddick, USA; 2004
Women: 130mph (210kph); Brenda Schultz-McCarthy, Holland; 2006 and Venus Williams, USA, 2008.

Oldest Number One

Men: Andre Agassi; 33 years 13 days; May 2003
Women: Martina Navratilova; 30 years 10 months; August 1987.

Youngest Number One

Men: Lleyton Hewitt; 20 years 10 months; November 2001
Women: Martina Hingis; 16 years 6 months; March 1997.

Go, cat, go!

The fastest land animal is the cheetah. It can reach a speed of 75mph (120kph) and it accelerates faster than a sports car. Narrowly built and covered with black spots, it roams the African prairies and uses its incredible speed to catch gazelles, springboks, and impalas. It can't run that fast for very far, though, so it needs to strike quickly.

The largest cat

Up to 13ft (4m) long and weighing as much as 650lb (300kg), tigers are the largest of all the big cats. Tigers live in the forests and jungles of Asia and their roars can be heard for up to 3 miles (5km). They are illegally hunted by some humans for their skins, and are becoming much rarer.

The longest snake

The longest snake in the world is the reticulated python. It is often about 20ft (6m) long and one example in Indonesia measured almost 33ft (10m). It lives in the rainforests of Southeast Asia and eats rodents, birds, and even pigs, killing its prey by constriction. The green anaconda from South America is almost as big as the reticulated python.

King of the swingers

The orangutan, which means "person of the forest," is the largest mammal that lives up in the trees. The males can grow up to over 5.5ft (1.7m) tall and tend to sleep on the ground, but the females make nests out of branches and leaves in the trees. There are two different species, the Bornean and the Sumatran, which are both from Southeast Asia. Like humans, orangutans have opposable thumbs, but they also have opposable big toes.

20
feet - the longest snake in the world

The bird with a huge beak

The Australian pelican's beak can measure up to 18.5in (47cm), and it can carry about 3gal (13.64l) of water depending on the size of the bird. The only bird designed to have a beak that is longer than its body is the South American sword-billed hummingbird. When it perches on a tree, it holds its beak vertical to reduce the strain on its neck.

Big-eared brain box

Famously, African elephants can be distinguished from Asian elephants because they have bigger ears, but there are several differences. The African elephant is bigger. It is the largest animal on land, growing up to 13ft (4m) tall and weighing 8 tons (7,500kg). The African elephant also has the biggest brain of all land mammals. Both types use their trunks to grip things, but Asian elephants have only one finger-like protrusion at the end of their trunks, whereas the African has two.

The planet's greatest ape

African gorillas are the biggest of all the apes in the world . They can grow up to 6ft (1.8m) tall and can weigh more than 400lb (181kg). Despite sometimes looking very fierce, African gorillas are quite gentle-natured vegetarians who like to groom and cuddle each other, and post little threat to humans. They have individual fingerprints, just like humans, and even know how to use tools such as a stick to measure the depth of water.

Elementary my dear Watson

Although many people had contributed to the development of the telephone, it was Alexander Graham Bell and his assistant Thomas Watson who arrived at the system of using a vibrating reed to transmit the voice, and took out the patent on the telephone in 1876.

Farmsworth to the fore

Who invented the television? The record now rests with an American, Philo Farmsworth. In 1923, American engineer Vladimir Zworkin invented and patented an electronic image scanner that allowed pictures to be stored as electrons ready for transmission (a crude TV camera). Then, in 1927, using a scanner developed by himself, Farmsworth transmitted pictures to a receiver for the first time – a TV set. At the same time, in 1925, Scottish electronics engineer John

Logie Baird demonstrated picture transmission at Selfridges department store on London's Oxford Street using equipment he'd designed himself. After a $50 million (£32.8 million) legal battle in 1930, Farmsworth claimed the patents.

The world's first CD

In 1979, Philips unveiled their CD system, in production in a German factory, delivering their first CD in 1982. The first commercial CDs pressed were "The Visitors" by Abba, and a recording of Herbert Von Karajan conducting "The Alpine Symphony" by Richard Strauss.

The World Wide Web

American computer boffin Joseph Licklider invented the Internet. First referred to as the Intergalactic Computer Network, he began developing the idea in 1962 and it took until 1965 to perfect.

Hello Dolly, Dolly

On 5 July 1996, Dolly the Sheep was born at Edinburgh University, the first animal cloned from an adult somatic cell. She lived to be seven years old.

Steaming ahead

The Chinese hold the record for the earliest steam-powered cars: as early as the 17th century, steam-powered cars were in use in China.

Jet setter

The jet engine, using a gas turbine to provide thrust, was invented by RAF aircraft engineer (Sir) Frank Whittle in 1930. Jet propulsion took off with the invention of the rocket by the Chinese in the 11th century.

Mass car production

When Henry Ford opened the first car factory assembly line to mass-produce the Model T Fords in 1908, he told prospective customers they could have any color they liked as long as it was black.

Radio gaga

The first radio transmission was in 1895, after Gugliemo Marconi adapted work that been pioneered by others during the previous 50 years. Gugliemo created the first commercially viable wireless telegraph system.

Cell phones

The first commercial cell phones went on sale in the US in 1983; they were solely analog transmission and came connected to a "portable," which was a unit the size of a small briefcase.

The first car engine

Swiss inventor Francois de Rivaz built the first internal combustion engine, which burned hydrogen and oxygen, and attached it to a vehicle in 1806. However, it wasn't until 1886 that German engineer Karl Benz – later to be of Mercedes Benz fame – created the first commercially viable vehicle powered by a four-stroke petrol-driven engine.

The first color transmission

In 1938 John Logie Baird invented the color TV when he broadcast a color image from his south London studio to a receiver set up in the Dominion Theatre in London's West End.

One small step for man...

American Neil Armstrong was the first man to set foot on the Moon on 20 June 1969, an event watched live on TV by a worldwide audience of 500 million people. This came 10 years after the first successful landing by an unmanned craft, which was the Russian mission *Luna-2* and it touched down on 12 September 1959.

The largest muscle

Out of the 650 muscles in the body, the largest muscle is in your bottom and is known as the gluteus maximus. Muscles turn energy into motion. Like a car engine, muscles are the "engine" that your body uses to work.

Human skin

Our skin is the largest organ of the integumentary system. The integumentary system, which protects the body from damage, consists of the skin, hair, nails, and sweat glands and their products – sweat and mucus. The term derives from the Latin word "integumentum," which means covering. The integumentary system cushions and protects the underlying muscles and organs, regulates body temperature, and is the location of sensory receptors for pain, pressure, and temperature. Our skin also helps synthesize vitamin D, when it is exposed to the sun.

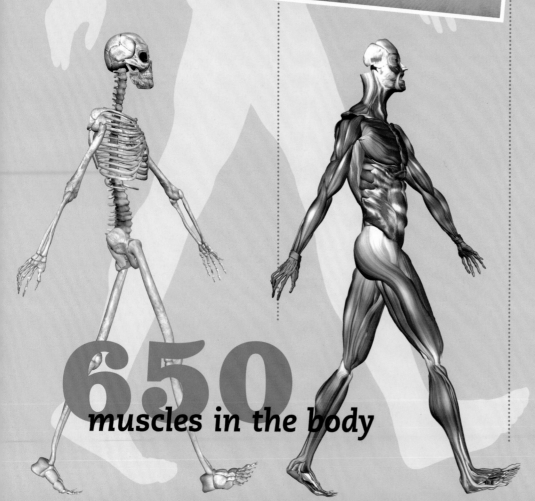

Record energy levels

If you yelled for eight years, seven months and six days, you would have produced enough sound energy to heat one cup of coffee.

650
muscles in the body

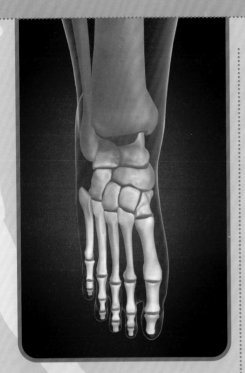

First ever inoculation

The earliest use of inoculation was in Chinese culture. From AD1000 the ancient

52
bones in the foot

Chinese practiced a form of immunization that involved inhaling dried powders derived from the crusts of smallpox lesions. Another method of inoculation was scratching the powder into their skin. In 1796, Edward Jenner of Gloucestershire, England, introduced the safer method of inoculation with the cowpox virus, a non-fatal virus that also induced immunity to smallpox. This led to smallpox inoculation falling into disuse and eventually being banned in England in 1840. Inoculations are still carried out today, against polio, tuberculosis, tetanus, influenza, and a number of other deadly viruses.

The red stuff

Blood type O, in humans, is by far the most common in virtually every racial group across the globe.

Bone idol

Your feet have more bones in them than any other part of the body. There are nearly 200 bones in the body but the feet contain 52 bones alone – in fact, the bones in your feet make up around one-quarter of all the body's bones. Your foot bones form three strong arches: two length ways, and one across your foot. Ligaments bind your bones together along with the tendons of your foot muscles. This means you can hold your foot firmly in the arched position, but still flex it.

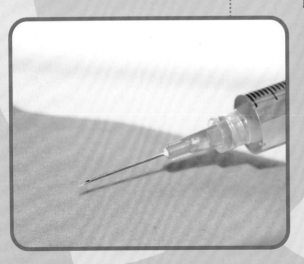

A typical person has around 8.5–10.5pt (4–5l) of blood in their body. Our blood carries oxygen and nutrients around our bodies to the cells, and picks up waste materials to take out of the body. Our blood contains antibodies to fight invading germs, while our heart is the pump that keeps the blood moving.

Nervous illnesses

Disorders of the brain and nervous system – around 1,000 of them – result in a greater number of hospitalizations than any other disease group, including cancer and heart disease. The human nervous system consists of around a hundred billion nerve cells – or neurons. Neurological illnesses affect more than 50 million Americans annually.

Busy brain

The brain is the only organ known to be more active at night than during the day. It turns out that when you turn off and sleep, your brain turns on – which defies logic as you would have thought all that moving around, thinking, working, and reading that's done on a daily basis would take more brain power. During sleep, your brain processes new memories, converts memory into more permanent or enhanced forms, hones skills, and even solves problems.

The first computer graphics

Westworld (1973) and follow-up *Futureworld* (1976) were the first mainstream movies to use 2-D and 3-D computer graphics. The first fully-fledged CGI character was Cindy in the 1981 movie *Looker*. *Toy Story*, in 1995, was the first feature-length fully-CGI animation.

The earliest movie

This was a two-second clip called *Roundhay Garden Scene*, created by Louis Lee Prince in Leeds, UK, in 1888. Seven years later, British

Highest-grossing film

Avatar holds the record with $267,976,702 (and growing). It cost around $237m to make and was nominated for nine Oscars in 2010.

28
Godzilla movies made in *fifty years*

electrician Robert Paul developed the projector, to start screening movies to large audiences.

How many Bonds?

James Bond is the longest running film franchise to date. Since *Dr. No* in 1962, there hav been six different official Bonds in the 22 movies: Sean Connery, George Lazenby, Roger Moore, Timothy Dalton, Piers Brosnan, and the current, Daniel Craig, who has played 007 twice.

The first talkie

The first movie to feature some synchronized sound and dialogue was *The Jazz Singer* in 1927, while *The Lights of New York*, which came out the following year, was the first all-sound movie.

The first modern movie

The Great Train Robbery (1903) is considered to be the first movie in the modern sense: it was 10 minutes long, with 14 different scenes.

The biggest movie franchise

Between its first appearance in 1954 and retirement in 2004, there were 28 Godzilla movies – the greatest number of movies made with a character that was created for the big screen. With *Quantum of Solace*, there will have been 22 James Bond movies, but this franchise is based on a character created for a book.

Harry hits the big screen

The *Harry Potter* series is the most financially successful movie franchise of all time. *Harry Potter and the Philosopher's Stone, the Chamber of Secrets, the Prisoner of Azkaban, the Goblet of Fire, the Order of the Phoenix,* and *the Half-Blood Prince* have amassed total box office takings of $5.4billion.

The most expensive movies ever made

In terms of what was actually paid out to create them, the record-breaking movies of all-time are as follows: *Pirates of the Caribbean: At World's End* – $300,000,000; *Avatar* – $280,000,000); *Spider-Man 3* – $258,000,000; and *Quantum of Solace* – $230,000,000. If you adjust for inflation to bring the cost of older movies up to today's figures, *War And Peace*, made in 1968, would be the most expensive at $700,000,000, and *Cleopatra*, made in 1963, would be in third place, at a cost of 295,000,000.

The most expensive movie franchise

This record goes to *Pirates of the Caribbean*. The three *Pirates* movies have cost a total of $665,000,000, at an average of $221,660,000 each, just ahead of the *Spider-Man* series, which cost $606,000,000, to give a per-picture average of $202,000,000.

The most Oscars

Three films share the record for most Oscars won: *Ben Hur* (1959), *Titanic* (1997), and *Lord of the Rings: The Return of the King* (2003), each winning 11 Oscars. However, movie buffs consider *Return of the King* to be the most successful of the trio. The film won every category it was nominated in: (Best Picture, Director, Adapted Screenplay, Original Score, Song, Visual Effects, Art Direction, Costuming, Make-up, Sound Mixing, and Film Editing).

Most successful animated movie

This record is held by *Shrek 2*, which took $919,838,758 around the world.

The Big Five Oscars

Three films have also won the "Big Five" Oscars of Best Picture, Director, Actor, Actress, and Writing. They are: *It Happened One Night* (1934); *One Flew Over The Cuckoo's Nest* (1975); and *The Silence of the Lambs* (1991).

Most successful golfer

American Sam Snead holds the record for the most PGA Tour titles won. Snead won an extraordinary 82 in a career that lasted from 1934 to 1979. Tiger Woods is third on the list with 65, behind Snead and Jack Nicklaus (73), but Tiger is the only one still playing, so watch this space! The golfer with the most wins on the LPGA Tour is Kathy Whitworth, who notched up 88 between 1958 and 1985.

Tiger's takings

For seven of the last 10 years, Tiger Woods has finished top of golf's earnings league with a total earning

over that time of over $71 million (£46.5 million). The highest earning British golfer over the same period is Colin Montgomerie, with around $9 millon (£5.9 million).

Longest PGA Tour winning streak

This honor goes to Bryan Nelson, who won 11 tournaments in a row in 1945. He won 18 times that year, and had seven second-place finishes.

Tiger time

In April 1997, at the tender age of 21, Tiger Woods became the youngest winner of The Masters in Augusta, Georgia, USA. His winning margin of 12 shots is a record that still stands today. He is also the youngest player to reach a number one world ranking. Woods was only 21 years, 24 weeks old when he achieved this. Bernhard Langer held the previous record – 29 years, 31 weeks, in 1986.

Golfspeak

The "bogey", the first stroke system in golf, was used in late 19th century England. In 1890, Hugh Rotherham of Coventry devised this "ground score" – the number of shots needed at each hole. Golfers believed they were playing a "Mr. Bogey" when measuring against this bogey score.

The biggest range

The biggest golf range in the world is in Joong-Ku, Korea, at the Sky 72 Golf Dream Club, which has 300 driving bays.

Scoring low

The lowest score on a round in a PGA Tour match is 63. This record is shared by seven golfers: Bruce Crampton (1975); Ray Floyd (1982); Gary Player (1984); Vijay Singh (1993); Michael Bradley (1995); Brad Flaxon (1995); Jose Maria Olazabal (2000); Mark O'Meara (2001).

The fastest golfer

The most golf balls hit in a minute was by American David Ogron who, in 2007, drove 102 balls set up for him by his caddy Scott McKinney. David also holds the record for most balls hit in two minutes (133), and the most hit in 24 hours (10,392) in 2002.

The oldest course

The oldest golf course in the world is the Old Links Golf Course in Musselburgh, Scotland, which dates back to the 16th century.

Where it all began

Although golf is usually thought to have originated in Scotland, there are recordings of a very similar game being played in China in the 11th century and in Holland in the 13th century. In Dutch, the word "golf" means stick or club.

Interplanetary driving

The longest ever golf drive was an estimated 2.2 billion yd (2.02 billion km)! Russian flight engineer Mikhail Tyurin took it during a space walk in 2006 – NASA estimated the ball would orbit the Earth for three days before burning up.

Tallest tree

The world's tallest tree is the Hyperion, in the Redwood National Park, near Eureka, California, USA. The redwood is 379.3ft (115.6m), over 8ft (2.5m) taller than the previous record holder "The Stratosphere Giant". These skyscraper trees are taller than New York's Statue of Liberty. One tree in Australia was reported at 374ft (114m) in the 1880s, but the record is in dispute. The second tallest, the Helios, at 375.9ft (114.5m), and third tallest the Icarus, at 371.2ft (113m), were also found in Eureka.

California dreaming

The world's tallest cactus is the cardon cactus (Pachycereus pringlei), found in the Sonoran Desert, Baja California, Mexico. It is an amazing 63ft (19.2m) tall and was found by two men on an expedition to find a towering

cactus in April 1995. The tallest home-grown cactus is the Cereus peruvianus, measuring 77ft (23.4m) in September 2009, and still growing. This record-breaking cactus was grown by the SDM College of Dental Sciences in Dharwad, Karnataka, India.

Oldest tree

The world's oldest tree is "Methuselah," which is 4,767 years old and grows in California's White Mountains in the US. Methuselah is a particularly amazing record breaker as it has lived for more than a millennium longer than any other tree found on our planet. Methuselah is a Bristlecone pine, which can be found in the US states of California, Nevada and Utah.

Rosy records

The world's largest rosebush is a white Lady Banksia from Tombstone, Arizona, USA. From a single trunk, it spreads over an arbor that covers 8,000sq ft (743sq m) and originated from a root in Scotland back in 1885. The rose with the most blooms is in Australia. A Cecile Bruener rose holds the record with 5,470 blooms and it was grown by Clifton Martin, of Merrylands, New South Wales, Australia, in 1982. Finally, the tallest self-supported rosebush measured 13ft 3in (4.03m) on 5 December 2005 and grows in San Diego, California, USA.

Tiny trees

The world's smallest tree is the Dwarf Willow and it lives in the frozen Arctic, usually growing in tundra and rocky moorland, at over 4,921ft (1,500m) altitude. It reaches the giddy heights of 2in (5cm) when it's fully grown but, though it doesn't grow tall, it does spread itself over the ground.

$266,667
paid for the most expensive bouquet

Most expensive bouquet

The world's dearest bouquet, made entirely out of one million Riyals – the currency of Saudi Arabia – folded into origami flowers, costs $266,667 (£177,624).

Tall flowers

Martien Heijms of Oirschot, the Netherlands, grew the tallest sunflower in the world in 1986. Its total height was 25ft 5in (7.76m). Just four years after the sunflower, a dahlia, grown by R. Blythe of Nannup, Western Australia, broke that record. It grew to a height of 25ft 7in (7.8m), which just beat the sunflower by 1.5in (4cm).

Flesh-eaters

The largest carnivorous plants are part of the Nepenthes family. These are large vines, which can grow up to 33ft (10m) long and plants in this genus can catch creatures such as frogs and even rodents. A plant is said to be carnivorous if it attracts, captures, and kills animal life-forms.

Fastest flesh-eater

The fastest-acting trap belongs to the underwater plants in the genus Utricularia, which suck prey into bladders in times as short as 1/30th of a second. However, the most gruesome flesh-eating plant has to be the famous Venus flytrap, which has leaf lobes that quickly capture prey in a really dramatic fashion.

Christmas trees

The biggest Christmas tree in the world, at 362ft (110.35m), was erected in Mexico City in 2009. Made of steel wires, it was covered in 1.2 million light bulbs and 50 miles (80km) of cable. This surpasses the previous record in Aracaju, Brazil, by 9.5in (24cm). Mayor Marcelo Ebrard led the lighting ceremony, as the Shola Cantorum Orchestra and the Mariachi Gama Mil Band played.

First to the South Pole

In 1911, Roald Amundsen (1872–1928), the Norwegian explorer, became the first person to reach the South Pole. Famously, he just beat the British explorer Captain Scott. Amundsen was one of the world's greatest explorers. He was the first person to navigate the Northwest Passage and he was the first to have been to both the North and South Poles.

Ground-breaking Cook

Captain James Cook (1728–79) from Britain was the first person to make a detailed exploration of the southern reaches of the Pacific Ocean. He was also the first European to circumnavigate New Zealand, land on the coast of eastern Australia, and visit Hawaii. Until then, people believed that there was just one, huge southern landmass, which they called the Terra Australis Incognito ("unknown southern land"). The Cook Islands are named after him.

Travels in China

Marco Polo (1254–1324) was an Italian trader and explorer and one of the first Europeans to travel to China. Amazingly, he was just 17 years old when he traveled from his homeland to the exotic eastern land. Marco Polo became the Emperor Kublai Khan's friend, and worked for him for 20 years, while also traveling round China. *Il Milone*, his account of his travels, became the best-known travel book in the world and was responsible for a new European interest in China.

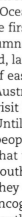

1953
year Mount Everest was first conquered

Potatoes and puddles

The British adventurer Sir Walter Raleigh (1552–1618) is credited with bringing the potato to Ireland and popularizing the use of tobacco. He was involved in British attempts to colonize America and also attempted to find El Dorado, "the city of gold" in South America. He is also famous for putting his cloak over a puddle so Queen Elizabeth I didn't have to get her feet wet.

Why Mexicans speak Spanish

Hernán Cortés Pizarro (1485–1547) was the leader of the Spanish colonization of the Americas. Pizarro traveled into territory that was completely unknown to Europeans when he marched across Mexico and conquered the Aztec Empire. He made Mexico part of Spain, and governed it himself in 1521–24.

Ultimate African adventurer

Until David Livingstone (1813–73), a Scottish missionary, started to explore Africa it had remained an almost completely unknown continent to the rest of the world. He was the first person to map huge parts of it and was the first European to cross southern Africa. No one heard from him for five years and he was presumed dead until an intrepid New York reporter called Henry Stanley finally found him in 1871, saying the famous greeting, "Dr Livingstone, I presume?".

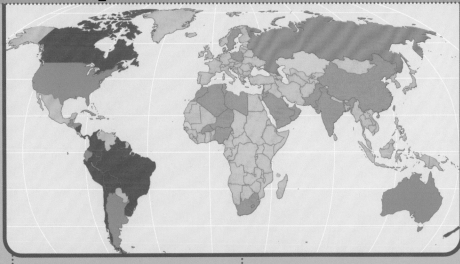

Scaling the heights

New Zealander Sir Edmund Hillary (1919–2008) and the Sherpa Tenzing Norgay (1914–86) reached the summit of Mount Everest on 29 May 1953. No one had ever managed to successfully reach the peak of the world's highest mountain before.

Everest without oxygen

On 8 May 1978, Mount Everest was finally conquered without the use of supplementary oxygen, by Reinhold Messner (b. 1944) and Peter Habeler (b. 1942). Many specialists thought they wouldn't be able to breathe properly and risked brain damage.

'Admiral of the Indian Seas'

Portuguese explorer Vasco da Gama (1460-1524) was the most successful in the European Age of Discovery. He led the first ships to sail directly from Europe to India and back, setting up a sea route to Asia that would help bring about European domination through sea power, commerce, and colonialism. The first Portuguese count not born a royal, da Gama died of malaria in Cochin, India.

First to build high

Stone buildings could not be built much higher than 500ft (152m) because they couldn't support their own weight and would topple over. Architects worked out how to use a steel frame to support buildings and this allowed really tall buildings to

be built for the first time in the late 19th century. The first steel-framed skyscraper was the Home Insurance Building in Chicago, which was later demolished. Completed in 1885, it was ten storeys high, reaching 138ft (42m).

The most skyscrapers

New York has the most freestanding skyscrapers over 500ft (152m) in the world. The Empire State Building 1,454ft (443.2m), built in 1931, is the tallest building in New York and is probably the most famous building in the world.

The best of British building

The oldest iron-framed building in the world is called The Flaxmill, and is located in Shrewsbury, England. Regarded as the forerunner to modern skyscrapers it was built in 1797, and is now owned by the English Heritage organization and is a listed building.

Paris reaches for the skies

Very high skyscrapers were banned from everywhere in the French capital except in La Défense district after the Tour Maine Montparnasse was built in 1972. The French authorities felt that having lots of tall buildings would spoil the Paris skyline. Times have changed though and permission has now been granted for the Tour Generali, an ecologically sound building in La Défense, which will become the tallest building in the European Union. It will be 1,100ft (318m) tall.

Growing up

New York has the most freestanding tall buildings, but Hong Kong is the densest skyscraper city. Often, several tall towers are clustered on the same base. Hong Kong is situated on islands so cannot expand outwards – it has to grow upwards! The International Finance Center is the city's tallest building (1,362ft/415m).

Tallest building in the world

The world's tallest building is the Burj Khalifa in Dubai, once known as the Burj Dubai. At 2,717ft (828m), it has over 160 stories, houses the world's highest swimming pool (on the 76th floor), and the world's

highest mosque (on the 158th floor). It is also the world's tallest free-standing structure. The record was previously held by Taipei 101, in Taipei, at 1,671ft (509m); followed by the Shanghai World Financial Center (1614ft/492m); and the Petronas Towers (1483ft/452m) in Kuala Lumpur, the world's tallest building for 6 years from 1998. The primary contractor for the Burj Khalifa, Samsung C&T of South Korea, also built the Taipei 101 and the Petronas Towers. Dubai is also home to the world's tallest hotel, the 72-story Rose Rayhaan Rotana, which stands at 1,093ft (333m).

Chicago reborn

Chicago had lots of early skyscrapers but, until the 1960s, height restrictions were placed on new buildings so it stopped competing with the other skyscraper cities of the world. Chicago has one of the tallest buildings in the world, the Sears Tower 1729ft (527m), and will soon have the tallest all-residential building, the Chicago Spire 2,000ft (610m), which will be completed in 2011.

Skyscrapers in the historical city

London is known as one of the greatest historical cities in the world, so there are strict restrictions on exactly what can be built there. Up until the 1960s, building heights were restricted to 100ft (30m). However, the English capital now has some very interesting skyscrapers. One of its tallest buildings is the 40-storey-high 30 St Mary's Axe, which was designed by world-famous architects Fosters & Partners. Situated in the heart of the city's financial district, it is also known as the Gherkin because of its unusual shape (curved both vertically and horizontally).

The first base jump

This took place in 1783, and it was the first parachute jump, too, when its inventor Louis-Sebastien Lenormand leapt from the 66ft (20m) high tower of the Observatory in Montpelier, France. Lenormand used a 14ft (4.25m) parachute with a rigid wooden frame.

Ride the skies

Sky surfing is a combination of freefall parachuting and snowboarding, in which the parachutist straps a board to his feet and freefalls standing up, performing tricks and spins on the way down. It is banned by

The highest bungee jump

Professional stuntman Curtis Rivers took a record-breaking jump of 49,869ft (15,200m) from a hot air balloon above Andalucia, Spain, in 2002. Curtis also holds the world record for the longest – in terms of duration – parachute jump: 45min, from a height of 25,000ft (7,620m). Curtis is famous for performing his amazing stunts on the big screen, too, having acted as a body double in movies such as *Tomorrow Never Dies* and *The Count of Monte Cristo*.

45

minutes – the longest parachute jump

Base jumping

The term "base jumping" means to parachute off a grounded object rather than out of a plane, and the name comes from what these objects might be:

Building
Antenna
Span (a bridge)
Earth (a cliff, mountain, or rock formation)

nearly every parachute club, not because of danger to the jumper but because there's a high risk of the board falling off and hitting someone else! In 1995, Xtreme Games gold medal winner Rob Harris was killed when his parachute got tangled while he was filming a commercial for a soft drink.

Fly like a bird

Paragliding is probably the nearest man is going to come to soaring like a bird as it holds the glider up by rising air currents, in exactly the same way birds stay aloft. The record for height gain – you always start off on a cliff or hilltop – is 14,650ft (4,526m) and was set by Robbie Whitall from the UK, in South Africa in 1993. The fastest paraglider was Charles Cazauk who flew at 25.57mph (41.15kph) in 2006, while the longest flight is 286.7 miles (461.6km) and was made by Frank Brown in Brazil in 2007 – that's just a little bit further than flying from London to Dublin in Ireland!

The greatest freefall jumps

The world records for the longest parachute freefall (4min 36sec), the fastest freefall (614mph/988kph), and the highest parachute jump (101,516ft/3,0942m), were all set by US Air Force Captain (later Colonel) Joseph Kittinger in 1960, when he jumped out of a hot air balloon (*The Excelsior III*) above the clouds over Ohio, USA.

Little tough guy

Most people assume that the strongest animal in the world is the elephant or the rhinoceros, but it's actually the rhinoceros beetle. Sometimes kept as a pet in Asia, this large scarab beetle can support 850 times its own bodyweight on its back, while an elephant isn't even able to lift its own weight.

A bat the size of a bee

The smallest mammal is the bumblebee bat, also known at Kitti's hog-nosed bat. It lives in western Thailand and Myanmar and only grows to be about 1.4in (3.5cm) long and weighs 0.7oz (2g). Etruscan pigmy shrews can weigh less than bumblebee bats, but they are usually slightly longer with a bigger skull.

As tall as a house

Giraffes are the tallest mammals, growing to a height of 18ft (5.5m). Their long necks and legs help them reach twigs and leaves that are out of reach for other animals in the African bush. The tuft at the end of their tails can be 3ft (1m) long – the longest hair on a mammal. Even though they are so tall, giraffes are not free from predators, because lions hunt them. Consequently, they can run extremely fast.

Bigger than the biggest dinosaur

The biggest animal that lived on Earth, including the dinosaurs, is the blue whale. They weigh up to 198 tons (180,000kg) and they can grow to over 100ft (30m) long, even though they feed almost exclusively on tiny sea creatures called krill. Despite their bulk, they can swim up to 30mph (48kph) when in danger. They also make the loudest animal sound, reaching 188 decibels – which is louder than a jumbo jet.

Woodpecker plays hide-and-seek

The ivory-billed woodpecker is the rarest animal in existence. It was believed to be extinct from the 1930s onwards because of the redevelopment of its natural habitat, but in 2005 a single male was found in the forests of Arkansas, USA. It is the largest woodpecker north of Mexico and has a black body with white

wing patches. Males have a red patch at the back of their crest. Research teams continue to try to find the bird again, but it is proving elusive.

A very, very long shoelace

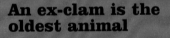

The longest animal ever recorded was a Lineus longissimus, commonly called a bootlace worm. In 1864, one measuring 180ft (55m) was washed up on the shore of St Andrews, Scotland. They are usually less than 0.4in (1cm) thick, but quite commonly reach a length of 100ft (30m).

Antelope in a hurry

At 75mph (120kph), the cheetah may be the fastest land mammal over a short distance, but it would easily be beaten by the pronghorn antelope for distances longer than 0.5 miles (800m). The antelope, resident in North America, can run at 35mph (56 kph) for 4 miles (6.4km), making it the fastest long-distance mammal, and knocking spots off the cheetah.

An ex-clam is the oldest animal

The oldest living animal was a clam discovered off the waters of Iceland

in 2007. The Arctica islandica, commonly called the ocean quahog, was between 405 and 410 years old, but unfortunately researchers killed the clam while cutting through its shell to find this out.

Early gamers

In the 1960s, computer technology was so primitive that only massive mainframe computers could support a gaming program. This meant the early gamers were students who had both the facilities and the time, and in 1961 a group from MIT in the US developed a very simple shoot 'em up game called Spacewar! This is acknowledged as the first computer game.

381

players at the largest computer game-in

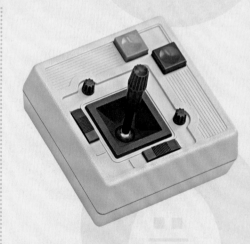

the end of 1972. This game is credited with kick-starting the whole video gaming revolution, as it achieved widespread popularity, first in arcades then, at the end of the decade, on home systems.

Spacewar!

Ten years later, in 1971, Spacewar! had evolved into the Galaxy Game, which became the first coin-operated video console game when it was instaled in the student common area.

The power of Pong

Pong, the table tennis-type video game, first appeared in arcades at

Invasion of the console games

At the end of the 1970s, Space Invaders became the most-played arcade game, generating over $500 million (£328 million). Pac Man, out in 1980, beat the record, selling over 350,000 units.

Getting involved

The leaps forward made in computer technology during the

late 1980s and 1990s saw much more power and control being delivered to home gaming units, meaning games became more like movies you took part in rather than games you played.

The youngest pro

In 2004, when American Victor de Leon, aka Lil Poison, was only six he decided to become a professional gamer. This made him the world's youngest ever pro.

Gaming goes home

The Atari 2600 console, released in October 1977, changed the face of home gaming as, using a microprocessor-based system, it could support more sophisticated games and graphics, while the joystick added to the gaming experience. Atari Corp. officially retired it on 1 January 1992, making it the longest-lived home video game console in gaming history.

The largest hand-held computer game-in

This took place in Sydney, Australia, in October 2007, when 381 people played on their Nintendo DS machines at the same time.

The largest arcade machine

You'll find this record-breaker in Los Angeles, USA. The arcade machine measures 13.5ft (4.11m) tall, 9.35ft (2.85m) deep, and 5.65ft (1.72m) wide. The screen is 72in (1.82m) and weighs 1,499lb (680kg).

The price of gaming

Current figures place the growing US gaming industry's sales at $12 billion (£8.17 billion). This is still a great deal less than the Hollywood movie business, but ahead of the music business which has been in decline, with sales of $9 billion (£6.13 billion) for the same period.

The biggest selling video game

The Super Mario Bros series, with total sales of $145 million (£95 million). The fastest completion of Super Mario Bros 3 was an amazing 11min 3sec, set by Freddy Andersson in July 2007.

Best-selling games console

The record is held by the PS2, which has sold a total of 120 million units worldwide since its release in 1997.

Most expensive game to create

This is Sega's Shenmue, which had a budget of $70 million (£46 million) and took seven years to create.

The most eagerly awaited computer game

Action game Grand Theft Auto 4 generated over $500 million (£328 million) in global receipts in its first week of release. By selling over six million units this beats the previous record of $300 million (£197 million) that was set by Halo 3 in 2007. The GTA series features the most celebrity guest stars of any game, including Ice T, Axl Rose, Chris Penn, and Dennis Hopper.

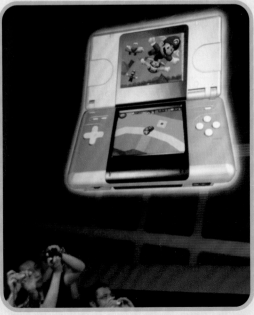

Heaviest brain

The heaviest human brain ever recorded weighed 5lb 1.1oz. (2.3kg). It belonged to a 30-year-old male, and was reported by Dr. T. Mandybur of the Department of Pathology & Laboratory Medicine at the University of Cincinnati, Ohio, in 1992. The average adult brain usually weighs 2.8–3lb (1.3–1.4kg) – a squirrel brain weighs around 0.2oz (6g).

Lightest brain

The world's lightest normal (nonatrophied) brain weighed just 1lb 8oz. (680g). It belonged to Daniel Lyon (Ireland), who died in New York, in 1907, age 46. He was just over 5ft (1.5m) tall and weighed 145lb (66kg).

Cleverest brain

The smartest person in the world is American Marilyn vos Savant, who in 1956 scored 228 in an IQ test when she was just ten years old.

Is fish the best food for your brain?

Neurotransmitters are made from amino acids found in protein foods such as fish. For brain cells to communicate effectively with each other to create neural pathways,

they require chemicals called neurotransmitters. Neurotransmitters are the "messengers" carrying messages from neuron to neuron. Fish is a food of excellent nutritional value, providing high-quality protein and a wide variety of vitamins and minerals, including vitamins A and D, phosphorus, magnesium, selenium, and iodine in marine fish. Oily fish, in particular, is rich in brain-boosting omega-3 polyunsaturated fatty acids. So, it really is true that eating fish can make you smarter.

Smartest criminals

It is rumored that the American Mafia leader Al Capone had an IQ of 200. An example of a criminal with a verified exceptional intelligence (IQ 170, at age ten) is the Unabomber Theodore Kaczynski. He was a successful researcher in mathematics before he turned against society.

Biggest neocortex

The proportion of the human brain devoted to the neocortex, the most complex part of the cerebral cortex, is larger than in all other mammals. This allows for cognitive skills and neural capacities superior to other animals. The human brain contains billions of nerves that simultaneously process information from our bodies, operate our internal organs, generate thoughts and emotions, store and recall memories, and control movement. In animals, the brain is the control center of the central nervous system, responsible for behavior. In mammals, the brain is located in the head, protected by

the skull, and close to the primary sensory apparatus of vision, hearing, equilibrioception (balance), sense of taste, and olfaction (smell).

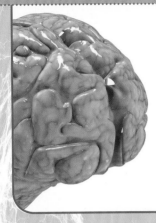

Right brain

People who use the right side of their brain are usually more creative, artistic, holistic, nonverbal, playful, emotional, intuitive, spontaneous, symbolic, and sociable. The lateralizations are functional trends, not always applicable.

Left brain

People who use the left side of their brain are more verbal, analytical, literal, linear, mathematical, rational, skeptical, closed, and cautious. However, no one is a "right brain only" or a "left brain only" person.

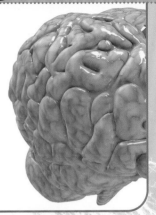

18
record days without sleep

hindbrain is made of the cerebellum, pons, and medulla. Often the midbrain, pons, and medulla are together referred to as the brainstem.

Home to most geniuses

Early 16th century Florence remains an unmatched example of having been home to the greatest number of artists at any one time: Leonardo da Vinci, Raphael, Michelangelo, and Botticelli being a few.

Sleep and the brain

The record for the longest period without sleep is 18 days 17hours,

Consciousness meter

In 2008, Steven Laureys, with colleagues from the University of Liege, Belgium, revealed for the first time how analysing the part of the brain responsible for day-dreaming may help separate the brain damaged from the brain dead, and thereby help predict coma recoveries.

Largest brain part

The cerebrum or cortex is the largest part of the human brain and is part of the "higher" brain function such as thought and action. The brain is made of three main parts: the forebrain, midbrain, and hindbrain. The forebrain consists of the cerebrum, thalamus, and hypothalamus (part of the limbic system). The midbrain consists of the tectum and tegmentum. The

set during a rocking chair marathon. The record holder, Maureen Weston, of Peterborough, Cambridgeshire, UK, set the record in April, 1977. She had hallucinations, paranoia, blurred vision, slurred speech, and memory and concentration lapses during that period. Sleep is necessary for your body and especially your brain. When you're asleep, the brain sorts through and stores information, replaces chemicals, and solves problems.

Most expensive paintings

By the end of 2007, six paintings had changed hands for more than $100 million (£65 million); the most expensive of them was simply titled No 5, 1948, by abstract expressionist artist Jackson Pollock, which was sold for $140 million (£92 million) at a private sale in 2006.

Da Vinci decoded

Fifteeth-century artist Leonardo da Vinci is best known for two of the most famous paintings in the world – *The Mona Lisa* and *The Last Supper* (which he painted directly on to the back wall of the dining hall of the Santa Maria delle Grazie convent in Milan, Italy). But Da Vinci was also

Fastest on the draw

The world record for saleable works is held by New York artist Morris Katz, who, in 1987, produced and

13,000
paintings produced by Pablo Picasso

Who painted the most?

Pablo Picasso is the most prolific of the modern masters, and it is estimated that during his 78-year career he produced over 13,000 paintings, 100,000 prints and engravings, 35,000 book illustrations, and 250 sculptures. The total value of everything he created is believed to be just fewer than $1 billion (£0.65 billion).

a renowned scientist, engineer, inventor, mathematician, anatomist, and architect. Among his concepts were a helicopter, solar power, the tank, and the calculator. He also lectured and wrote about civil engineering and plate tectonics.

sold an extraordinary 103 paintings in 12 hours. Katz is also the world record holder for the fastest saleable painting. In 1988 he painted a 12 x 16in (30.5 x 40.6cm) canvas of a child in the snow in 30 seconds flat, and sold it on the spot.

First chronicled

Michelangelo – painter, sculptor, architect, poet, and engineer – was the first Western artist whose biography was published while he was still alive. In fact, two biographies were published in his lifetime. He is also the best-documented artist of the 16th century. The *Pietà* and *David*, two of his best-known sculptures, were completed before he was 30. In his personal life, he was abstemious and once said to his apprentice, Ascanio Condivi: "However rich I may have been, I have always lived like a poor man."

which were to be a considerable influence on the impressionist movement, and left behind a legacy of some of the most recognizable and valuable paintings ever, including *Vase With Twelve Sunflowers*, *Wheat Field With Crows*, and *The Starry Night*.

The most instantly recognizable painting

This is the *Mona Lisa*, which hangs in Le Louvre in Paris. Featuring a lady called *Lisa del Giocondo*, it was commissioned from Leonardo da Vinci by her husband Francesco, a wealthy Italian merchant, in 1503. However, the painting took several years, with Da Vinci finishing it just before his death in 1519. The painting's full title is Portrait of Lisa Gherardini, wife of Francesco del Giocondo.

Two in Top 10 list

Dutch artist Vincent Van Gogh painted two of the ten most expensive paintings sold at auction. During the 19th century, Van Gogh developed the impressionist and neo-impressionist techniques

Largest volcano

The world's largest active volcano is Mauna Loa in Hawaii, which has erupted 40 times in the last 150 years. Mauna Loa is 13,677ft (4,169m) above sea level and from its base below sea level to its summit Mauna Loa is taller than Mount Everest.

Volcanic eruptions

The longest ever eruption from a volcano has lasted 5,000 years – and is still going on! Some geologists claim that Stromboli, in Italy, has been active for all that time and that's one of the reasons why the volcano has been

Highest temperature

When basalt rock (the most common volcanic rock) erupts under water, it tends to erupt at a temperature of between 1,150–1,200°C (2,102–2,192°F). This is the highest temperature reached either under water or on dry land. There are more than 1,500 active volcanoes on Earth and at least 80 of them are under the oceans.

Highest volcano

Ojos del Salado in Chile is the world's highest volcano. It is located in the Andes mountain range and stands at 28,435ft (6,887m). Mount Fuji in Japan is probably the world's most famous volcano, and stands at 12,388ft (3,776m). Fuji is a dormant volcano but has erupted at least 16 times since AD781. The last time it erupted was in 1707.

Fastest flow

The fastest ever lava flow was from Mount Nyiragongo in the Democratic Republic of the Congo, Africa. On 10 January 1977 the crater walls of the volcano fractured and lava flowed down the flanks of the mountain at 60mph (97kph).

New volcanoes

The "newest" volcano was discovered in 1973 on the island of Heimaey in Iceland. New volcanoes form every century, but usually in the same area as existing volcanoes. In 1943, a volcano was discovered growing in the middle of a flat cornfield in Mexico. Paricutin grew to 1,353ft (412m) and erupted for nine years. Today it is 9,213ft (2,808m) above sea level.

Highest spurt

The highest distance reached by fountains of lava was around 4,920ft (1,500m) high on the island of Izu Oshima, Japan, in 1968. However, the explosive eruption plumes generated at volcanoes such as Pinatubo, near the Philippines, was 147,600ft (45km).

referred to as the "Lighthouse of the Mediterranean". In general, eruptions last as long as there is magma and sufficient pressure coming of the ground. About 50% of eruptions last less than two months and only 17% of eruptions last longer than one year.

The first recorded volcano

The first recorded volcano was in 475BCE at Mount Etna in Sicily. Since that period it has erupted more than 250 times. In 1979 a new crater opened up without warning and erupted.

1,500 active volcanoes on Earth

The most deadly volcano

The deadliest volcano of all time was Tambora on Sumbawa Island, Indonesia, which killed more than 88,000 people in 1815. Most died as an indirect result of the heavy ash fall, which blanketed the growing crops and polluted the water supplies over a wide region, including several neighboring islands.

Extinct volcanoes

Volcanoes can eject material at speeds of 2000mph (3219kph) but when nothing comes out, people think they're extinct. The Fourpeaked Volcano in Alaska was considered extinct as it had not erupted since 7,994BCE – however, it became active again in September 2006. An extinct volcano is a volcano which is not currently erupting and is not considered likely to erupt in the future – but, like the Alaskan example, who knows when a volcano may start to erupt again?

Beach volleyball

Beach volleyball, which was first introduced to the Olympics in 1996, is played on sand with two players per team. Since the sport gained huge popularity in the 1980s, countries with a strong beach culture have dominated – Brazil and the US, with Australia coming up behind. Remarkably, though, landlocked Switzerland is starting to have success at international level.

Best fast bowler

This record is held by Courtney Walsh of the West Indies. Walsh has taken a total of 519 Test wickets, at an average of 24.44 per Test.

Biggest rugby win

Argentina beat Paraguay by 152 points in May 2002. It is the biggest winning margin in an international game.

Rugby Premiership

The record number of tries scored by one person in the English Premiership, is six, by Australian Ryan Constable of Saracens, in 2000. The most tries scored in a career is 75, by Sale Shark's Steve Hanley, between 1998 and 2006. Tom Voyce of Wasps had the fastest try in 2004, when he touched down against Harlequins a mere 9.43 secs into the game.

Batting records

Brian Lara of the West Indies) holds the record for most Test Match runs scored at 11,953, between 1990 and 2007. He has since retired from Test cricket. The highest-scoring Englishman is Geoff Boycott, who scored 8,114 during his career.

Brian Lara also holds the record for the highest individual Test score with the 400 he made against England in St John's, Antigua, during the 2003/04 series. The highest scoring Englishman is Len Hutton, who made 364 against Australia at the Oval in 1938.

Lara also holds the record for most runs scored in one over: 28 (4-6-6-4-4-4) against South Africa in Johannesburg in 2004.

Best spin bowler

This record is held by Muttiah Muralitharan (Sri Lanka), who took 735 Test wickets, at an average of 21.95 per Test.

Fastest Test century

The world's quickest Test century was made by Viv Richards of the

West Indies who hit 56 balls against England in St John's, Antigua, in the 1985–86 series.

Most wicket-keeping Test Match catches

Mark Boucher of South Africa took 376 catches in 102 cricket matches during 1997–2007.

Rugby god

As well as scoring that famous "last minute of extra time" drop goal against Australia to win the 2003 Rugby World Cup for England, Jonny Wilkinson is England's youngest ever player, making his debut at 19. Wilkinson also holds the record for Test Match drop goals (29), and for Test Match points scored (1099). He has scored more Rugby World Cup points than anybody else (249), holds the record for most English Premiership points (1442), has scored the most points in a single Six Nations series (89), and is the only player ever to score points in two World Cup Finals.

Six of the best

During the 2007 Cricket World Cup, South Africa's Herschelle Gibbs became the only player in history to hit six sixes in one over. Herschelle's record took place in in St Kitts in the West Indies, against the inexperienced Netherlands team. The unfortunate bowler was Daan Van Bunge.

The greatest all-round cricketer

Jacques Kallis (South Africa) is the only cricketer in the history of the game to have scored more than 8000 runs, taken 200 wickets, and 100 catches in both Test Matches and One Day Internationals. He has scored 30 Test Match centuries – one more than Sir Donald Bradman – and in 2007 scored five centuries in four Test matches. He was Leading Cricketer in the World in the 2008 edition of *Wisden*.

Walking in space

Alexei Leonov (b. 1934) went one important step further than Yuri Gagarin on 18 March 1965 when he left his spacecraft, *Voskhod 2*, and became the first person to walk in space. His spacesuit enlarged and he had to let air out of it so that he could get back inside!

Women in space

Valentina Tereshkova (b. 1937) was rocketed up into space in the *Vostok 6* spacecraft on 16 June 1963. She became the first woman in space and orbited the Earth 48 times. The first female space tourist was an Iranian, Anousheh Ansari (b. 1966), who on 18 September 2006 paid $20 million (£13 million) to fly up to the International Space Station.

Gagarin goes into space

The Russian cosmonaut Yuri Gagarin (1934–68) became the first person in space when he manned the Soviet *Vostok 1* mission on 12 April 1961. The flight returned to Earth safely but unfortunately Gagarin was to die on a routine training flight just seven years later.

437
record days spent on a space station

The first man on the Moon

The Soviets led the early adventures in space, but the Americans were the first to land on the Moon. On 20 July 1969, Neil Armstrong (b. 1930) stepped out of the *Apollo 11* on to the Moon's surface and became the first man ever on the moon, saying the words, "That's one small step for man, one giant leap for mankind."

Round and round the Earth

Russian cosmonaut Valeri Polyakov (b. 1942) was launched into space on 8 January 1994 and stayed on the Mir space station for 437 days. He orbited the Earth more than 7,000 times before returning on 22 March 1995. This is the longest manned spaceflight in history.

Lunar scientist

Apollo 17 hosted the first scientist-astronaut to land on the Moon; Harrison H. Schmitt and his crew remained on the Lunar surface for 75 hours. This is the longest time that anyone has spent on the Moon. The Apollo missions represented the first and the last of the Moon landings.

Furthest from the Earth

American astronauts Jim Lovell (b. 1928), Jack Swigert (1931–82), and Fred Haise (b. 1933), the crew of the *Apollo 13*, have flown further from the Earth than any other humans. On 15 April 1970, their spacecraft reached a distance of 248,655 miles

Continuous human presence in space

Russia had a continuous human presence on the Mir space station from 5 September 1989 to 28 August 1999 – almost 10 years. The Mir, too old to use, was deliberately

Space disaster

Space travel is extremely dangerous. The worst ever space accident happened on 1 February 2003 when the space shuttle *Columbia* disintegrated while re-entering the Earth's atmosphere and all seven crew died.

(400,171km) from the Earth. That's a long way from home. A terrible disaster was averted when an explosion damaged the spacecraft. Jim Lovell famously said, "Houston, we've had a problem", but against all the odds the crew was able to return safely to Earth.

destroyed in 2001 as it re-entered the Earth's atmosphere. Russia, the USA, the EU, Canada, and Japan have jointly maintained the International Space Station, the largest ever, which, if all goes well, will break Mir's record for continuous, manned space occupation on 23 October 2010.

Most widely spoken

English is more worldwide in its distribution than any other spoken language, with 400 million native speakers, and 470 million to over a billion second language speakers. The main language in over 100 countries, it is by international treaty the language for aerial and maritime communication, official language of the UN, the global language of communications, science, technology, and diplomacy.

First written languages

No one knows exactly, but evidence from Harappa shows that the Indus Valley civilization in Asia had a written language by 3,500BCE. Writing from 3,400BCE has been found in an Egyptian tomb, and the Mesopotamian people in modern-day Iraq were writing by about 3,000BCE.

The youngest language

Afrikaans is believed to be the most recently developed natural language in the world. Afrikaans is spoken by over six million people worldwide, mainly in South Africa and Namibia, with smaller numbers in Botswana, Swaziland, Angola, Zimbabwe, and Lesotho. Afrikaans developed from Dutch, when Dutch settlers landed in South Africa in 1652. It was considered to be a Dutch dialect until the late 19th century, when it began to be regarded as a language in its own right. One-third of South Africans speak Afrikaans.

Most successful revival

The most successful example of language revival is Hebrew, which is once again in daily use in Israel. Languages are dying out all the time as communities become absorbed by other cultures. There are about 165 indigenous languages in North America, but more than 10,000 people speak only 8 of them. The elders speak about 75 and those languages will die with them.

2,500
words added to the English language every year

Do you speak Esperanto?

Esperanto is the most widely spoken made-up language in the world. It was devised by Ludwig Zamenhof in 1887 and is based on a mixture of many languages including Latin, German, English, French, Spanish, and Italian. With up to two million fluent speakers, it is the most popular made-up language, unless you are a fan of *The Lord of the Rings*, when you might prefer Elvish.

The world's largest vocabulary

The language with the most words is English – and it is getting bigger. Some people estimate that there may be as many as 1 million words in the English language, but only about 10 per cent of those are regularly used. About 2,500 new words are added to the most comprehensive dictionaries every year, and that does not include a lot of new scientific words and trademarks.

Largest and smallest alphabets

Khmer, which is the official language of Cambodia, has the largest alphabet in the world, with 74 letters. Khmer is spoken by about 12 million people in Cambodia, and by small numbers elsewhere in Asia. The language with the smallest alphabet is Rotokas, which is spoken by around 4,300 people in a particular area of Papua New Guinea. The Rotokas alphabet has just 12 letters.

Unusual ways of writing

Not all languages are written from left to right like English. Arabic, Hebrew, and many old Middle Eastern languages are written from right to left. Languages such as Japanese, Chinese, and Korean are written from right to left as well, but they are also written vertically rather than horizontally.

Many different languages

Papua New Guinea has the largest variety of languages within one country in the world. The population of just under 7 million people, between them, speak over 850 different languages.

The biggest killer of all

The biggest killer of humans is not a large animal. It is the little mosquito, no more that 0.5in (1.3cm) long, which transmits malaria to 190–350 million people every year, resulting in 1–3 million deaths. The 2nd leading cause of death in Africa after AIDS, the mosquito spreads disease from person to person when it punctures the skin for blood.

Man-eating lions

Lions rarely choose to attack and kill humans, but some get a taste for us and become man-eaters. In Tanzania, Africa, lions kill over 100 people every year. In Zambia, a man-eater christened The Cunning One set a personal record, eating 43 villagers. A lion is exceptionally strong and can drag a whole zebra carcass by itself. Cooperation within a pride of lions is legendary.

The killer whale

Killer whales, also called orcas, are the most powerful predators in the world. They hunt in packs like wolves and eat up to 500lb (227kg) of food a day. They kill otters and seals by throwing them in the air, slapping them, and head-butting them. They will also attack and kill other types of whales by preventing them from surfacing for air.

Roaming wild

Wild boar has the widest natural range of any hoofed mammal in the world. It was originally found in Britain, but has spread throughout all of Europe (except Scandinavia), North Africa, the Middle East, most of Central Asia, to China, Taiwan, and Japan. It is also found in Australia, Southeast Asia, and the Indonesian islands of Sumatra and Java.

The deadly snake

The hymadryad cobra, known as the king cobra, which grows to 18ft (5.5m), is the world's largest poisonous snake. The amount of neurotoxins it delivers in one bite can kill 20-30 grown men, or even an elephant. A mother king cobra, though fiercely protective, goes out to find prey to avoid instinctively eating her young.a pride of lions is legendary.

World's most lethal bears

Contrary to popular belief, bears do not like to hug their victims to death. Instead, they bite them or hit them with their front paws. Black bears and brown bears (including the grizzly bear) are the most dangerous to humans. They have killed over 50 people each in North America over the last century. Polar bears will attack

100
people killed yearly by lions in Tanzania

Shark attack!

In one of the first recorded and most famous shark attacks with multiple victims, four people were killed when swimming off the coast of New Jersey, July 1916. However, contrary to what many people think, sharks rarely try to attack humans. On average, there are only 4–5 fatalities from shark attacks each year. Sharks are good predators because they are fast, have sharp teeth, and have the best sense of smell of all fish. They can detect one part blood in 100 million parts of water.

Poisonous spiders

Very few spiders are poisonous – even a tarantula bite is unlikely to kill you. However, the black widow is a real killer. It kills more humans than any other spider, using its fangs to inject its venom, which is 15 times stronger than that of a rattlesnake.

humans, too, but they are much more interested in attacking other animals, such as seals. Polar bears are the only bears that are carnivorous, and they will club seals when they stick their heads above water and even throwing blocks of ice at them to stun them.

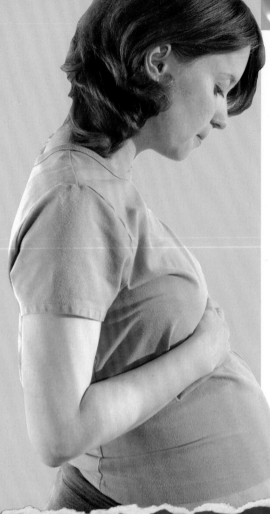

The smallest baby in the world

The lightest baby ever to survive weighed 8.6oz (244g), less than a can of soft drink. Born in Chicago, USA, in February 2005, the baby girl, who was named Rumaisa Rahman, was 1.3oz (37g) lighter than the previous record holder.

Lightest pairs

The world's lightest twins, Courtney (12oz/340g) and Chloe (12.5oz/354.4g) Smith of Alexandria, LA, with a combined weight of 24.5oz (694.5g), were born on March 1, 2000. Two sets of parents shared the record previously, at 30.33oz (860g). Roshan (17.28oz/490g) and Melanie (13.05oz/370g) were born to Katrina Gray in Brisbane, Australia, on November 19, 1993, while Wendy Morrison gave birth to Anne (14.81oz/420g) and John (15.52oz/ 440g) in Ontario, Canada, on 14 January 1994.

250,000
neurons forming in a baby's brain per minute

The biggest baby

The heaviest baby weighed 23.12lb (10.8kg), born to Anna Bates of Canada in 1879. The baby boy was 76cm (30in) long but sadly died 11 hours later. The heaviest baby to survive birth was also a boy. He weighed 22lb 8oz (10.2kg) in Aversa, Italy, in September 1955.

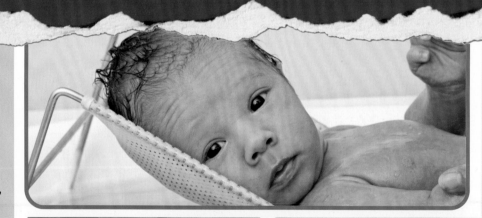

Multiple births

The most common form of human multiple birth is twins, but cases of higher orders have been recorded. The first surviving octuplets, the Chukwu/Udobi babies, were born in Houston, Texas, USA, on 20 December 1998.

Calm down, baby!

The pacifier, or dummy, was invented around 1900 in the USA. Soon it took the place of a thumb for millions of babies. In Britain in the mid-1800s, a forerunner called the "elastic gum ring" was used.

Most popular baby names

Jack has retained its position as the most popular boy's name in the UK. The American current favorite is

Jacob, followed by Michael and Ethan. Meanwhile, Emma has climbed to top position among popular girls' names in the US as Emily, a favorite since 1996, has slipped to number three. Between 1908 and 1961, the most popular girl's name in the US was Mary. The most popular girl's name in the UK is Olivia, which has climbed up from number three, Grace having dropped to fourth position.

A baby's brain

When we are babies, our brains are developing faster than at any other time in our lives. There is still a lot of mystery surrounding the development of the brain in early years, but scientists do know that just four weeks into gestation, the first brain cells, the neurons, are already forming at an astonishing rate: 250,000 every minute.

Fastest man on the planet

The fastest human being in the world is Jamaican "lightning bolt" Usain Bolt, who improved his own 100m and 200m world records to 9.58 and 19.19 seconds respectively at the 2009 World Championships.

Fastest woman on the planet

Florence Griffith-Joyner, whose 1988 world records for the 100 meters and 200 meters still stand at 10.49 seconds and 21.34 seconds respectively, remains the fastest woman sprinter in history. Griffith-Joyner, known as "Flo-Jo," was instantly recognizable for her trademark long, multi-colored fingernails. She brought glamor to the track, winning three Olympic and one World Championship gold medal for sprinting and the 4x100m relay. She died suddenly in her sleep in 1998, from an epileptic seizure.

The quickest man over distance

The legendary Ethiopian Haile Gebrselassie holds the world record for the Marathon (2hr 3min 59sec) – set at the 2008 Berlin Marathon. He also holds the records for 20km (55min 48sec); the 10km (26min 31 sec); and the One Hour Race, in which he ran 21.285km.

King Carl

The greatest sprinter of modern times is undoubtedly the American Carl Lewis. In a 15-year career from 1981 to 1996 he won five Olympic and four World Championship gold medals. Lewis managed to break or equal the US record for the 100 meters seven times, broke the world record for the 100 meters twice (9.92sec in 1988 and 9.86sec in 1991) and was anchor man in the 4x200m relay that set a world record in 1994 – 1min 18.86sec, which still stands – and the 4x100m relay that set the world record of 37.40sec in 1992. Carl Lewis became only the second athlete in history to win four consecutive Olympic gold medals in the same event when he won the Long Jump in 1984, 1988, 1992, and 1996, the indoor world record for which category Lewis still holds.

Fastest woman over distance

Britain's Paula Radcliffe holds the women's world records for the Marathon: 2h 15min 25 sec, set at

the London Marathon in 2003; and the 10km: 30min 21sec. Radcliffe took a long time to get into her stride, however, and was a good, but not great, middle-distance for several years before breaking through with world-beating performances. She currently holds ten world records – including the European Cross-Country – and was awarded an MBE in June 2002.

First Olympic sub-11 second female sprint

The first woman to run the 100 meters in under 11 seconds at an Olympic Games was American Evelyn Ashford in 1984. In total, Ashford managed to break the magic 11-second barrier 30 times, in a career that spanned five Olympic Games.

The greatest ever 400m hurdler

The legendary American athlete Ed Moses, who won gold medals for the 400 meters hurdles at the 1976 and 1984 Olympics, and the 1983 and 1987 World Championships, would work his leg muscles so hard during a race that, afterwards, he would stand in a large garbage bin full of ice to cool them down. Moses was unbeaten between 1977 and 1987.

Most sprint golds at the World Championships

Sprint legend Michael Johnson holds the men's record for the most sprint golds at the World Championships with nine (two for the 200 meters; four for the 400 meters; and three for the 4x400m relay). Representing the women is Gail Devers with a total of five World Championship golds (one for 100 meters; three for 100 meters hurdles; and one for 4x100m relay).

Three world records in 45 minutes

On 25 May 1935, in Detroit, Michigan, USA, American sprint king Jesse Owens achieved an amazing feat: he set three world records and equaled a fourth in just 45 minutes. His incredible sequence of records went like this: 3.15pm, 100yd, 9.4sec; 3.25pm, long jump, 8.13m; 3.45pm, 220yd, 20.3sec; 4pm, 220yd hurdles, 22.6sec.

The biggest South American population

By far the biggest country in terms of population in South America is Brazil, with over 190 million inhabitants. Colombia is in second place, with a population of over 44 million, followed by Argentina, which has 40 million. Brazil covers almost 3.3 million sq miles (8.5 million sq km), which is equivalent to almost half the land of the entire South American continent.

Most densely populated US state

New Jersey, located in the north-eastern United States, is the continent's most crowded state, with 1,174 residents per sq mile (453 per sq km).

Big bucks

The US economy is the biggest in the world. It had a gross domestic product (GDP) of $14.26 trillion in 2009. As well as having huge technological and manufacturing industries, it produces a lot of the world's salt and oil. The GDP of South America is $4.1 trillion. It is the world's biggest producer of coffee, cocoa, and bananas.

440
native languages in South America

The Amazon rainforest

The Amazon rainforest, made up of territories from nine different South American nations, is the largest rainforest in the world, covering 2.12 million sq miles (5.5 million sq km). More than a third of all plant and animal species can only be found there, including over 2.5 million insect species and more than 438,000 species of plants of social and economic interest. One in five of all birds in the world live in the rainforests of the Amazon.

The cold cold north

Alaska is by far the largest state in the US – much larger than Texas or California. It also has more coastline than all the other states combined. The smallest state by area is the District of Columbia, at just 68.3 sq miles (177 sq km).

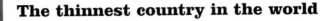

Mexico's largest ancient city

Teotihuacán, which is located in the Valley of Mexico, Central America, was the most advanced area of the Americas before the European colonization. Teotihuacán was a vast capital city with as many as 200,000 inhabitants in AD200–400. In fact, it was the largest city in the Americas and may have been even larger than Rome during the same period. Of course this is nothing compared to today's largest cities.

The thinnest country in the world

Considering how long it is, Chile is the thinnest country in the world. It is a strip that runs along the Pacific coast for more than half the entire length of South America. Chile is 2,670 miles (4,300km) long, but on average it is just 110 miles (175km) wide.

Most widely spoken language

Portuguese is the most widely spoken language in South America, even though it is only spoken in one country, Brazil. All the other countries of South America have Spanish as an official language except Surinam, which has Dutch; Guyana, which has English; and French Guyana, which has French. South America has over 440 native languages, whose history goes back to before European colonization. Some are becoming extinct, but Quechua is still spoken by 6 to 8 million people.

Oh Canada!

Canada is the biggest country in the Americas. It is 3.85 million sq miles (9.98 million sq km); the US is 3.79 million sq miles (9.83 million sq km). The population of the US, is, however, far higher.

Canadian inventors

Canadians have invented many of the simple things that we now take for granted. Henry Woodward invented the electric filament light bulb in 1874, but he sold the idea to Thomas Edison; James Naismith invented basketball in 1891; and Harry Wasylyk and Larry Hansen invented the green plastic disposable garbage bag in 1950.

Most crowded city

Sao Paolo in Brazil is the most populated city in South America, and is also one of the most polluted. With a population of over 11 million people, Sao Paolo is also the continent's richest city.

Potter's progress

The Harry Potter series has sold over 400 million copies of seven different titles, and with the merchandize, movies, and forthcoming Harry Potter theme park, the brand is worth $15 billion (£9.8 billion) worldwide. Harry has made author J.K. Rowling the world's first billionaire author. When *Harry Potter and the Goblet of Fire* was first put on sale in the US, the publishers had to hire 9,000 trucks to deliver it to the stores on time; and first print run was a record-shattering 3.8 million copies. *Harry Potter and the Order of the Phoenix* had an initial printing of 8.5 million, *The Half-Blood Prince* notched up 10.8 million, while *The Deathly Hallows* – released globally in 93 countries – sold 15 million copies in the first 24 hours.

Book early

The first commercially available books in the Western world came about after Johannes Gutenburg invented the printing press in 1436. Until then, books were hand lettered on parchment and would cost the same amount of money to buy as a small farm. In 1455, the 42-line Gutenberg Bible was published.

Middle Earth; higher sales

J.R.R. Tolkien is the only author with two entries in the Top 10 world best sellers – *Lord of the Rings* is fifth, with estimated sales of over 150 million, and is the highest-selling work of fiction; *The*

904
books written by Mary Faulkner

Hobbit is eighth with over 100 million copies.

The biggest-selling book in the world

The Bible, the only book believed to have sold over a billion copies, is the biggest-selling book to date. Sales estimates put its total sales at between five and six billion copies.

Most translated book

The full Bible is available in 438 different languages, including Afrikaans, Pashto (an Iranian language), Japanese, Tongan, and even Klingon.

The biggest literary franchise

This honor goes to the tales of Jessica and Elizabeth Wakefield in the *Sweet Valley High* series, which was created by Francine Pascal and which now runs to 400 titles and combined sales figures of 250 million.

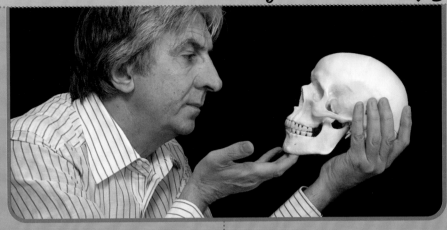

The most translated author

William Shakespeare is not the most translated author as many would believe, but science fiction author and Scientologist Ron L. Hubbard, whose work has been translated into 71 different languages. William Shakespeare's 39 plays have been translated into every major, living language.

The most prolific fiction authors

Romantic fiction writer Mary Faulkner holds the record at 904 novels. The South African writer used many pseudonyms, including Margaret Cameron, Molly Richmond, even the male *nom de plume* Hugh Desmond. Not far behind Mary Faulkner is another romantic novelist, Barbara Cartland, who published her first novel in 1925. Over the next 75 years she churned out 700 books – until her death in 2000. Her books had combined sales of almost one billion, an average of nine books a year. However, this astonishing output that, during the 1970s, saw 20 titles a year published under her name, prompted accusations that she might not be writing them all herself. She always strongly denied this and the accusations have never been proven.

Longest novel

Marcel Proust's *A la Recherche du Temps Perdu* (*Remembrance of Things Past* in English) is the longest conventionally read novel, at around 1.5 million words, in 13 volumes.

The best-selling author of all time

English crime writer Agatha Christie, who, between 1920 and 1973 wrote 80 detective thrillers that between them have sold around four billion copies – ten times more than the entire Harry Potter series.

Biggest ice sheet

The Antarctic ice sheet is the world's largest, containing 11.5 million sq miles (30 million sq km) of ice over an area of almost 5.5 million sq miles (14 million sq km). The Arctic ice cap has about 7.2 million cubic miles of ice, and about 58% of all the fresh water on the planet. During the winter, the Arctic ice pack in the North Pole grows to the size of the US. In summer, up to half the ice disappears.

World's largest glacier

The world's largest glacier is the Lambert glacier in Antarctica at the South Pole. It measures 60 miles (97km) wide and 250 miles (402km) long. This large land mass is located at around 3,100 miles (4,988km) southwest of Perth, in Australia. The rugged mountain ranges that flank the glacier, along with much of the rest of the frozen continent, are still largely unexplored. The Antarctic Treaty of 1959 reserves the continent for peaceful, non-political exploration and development.

Earliest life at the poles

Dinosaurs once roamed the harsh icy landscapes of both the Arctic and Antarctic: a tyrannosaur was found on Bylot Island, north of Baffin Island, which dated from some 70 million years ago. In the Antarctic, researchers have discovered the fossil remains of a plant-eating dinosaur which dates from about 200 million years ago.

Freezing point

The lowest temperature ever recorded on Earth was a terrifying -89.2°C (-129°F). This was measured at the Russian Base Vostok in Antarctica on 21 July 1983. The warmest recorded temperature there is -12.2°C (10.4°F). Antarctica holds the record for being not only the coolest place on earth but also the wettest place on the planet.

Highest continent in the world

Antarctica is the Earth's highest continent, with an average elevation of 7,500ft (2,300m). North America, in comparison, has an average elevation of 2,363ft (720m). The highest point in Antarctica is Vinson Massif at 22,481ft (4,897m). The lowest is the Bentley Subglacial Trench at 8,383ft (2,555m) below sea level. Antarctica is also the planet's fifth largest continent in area.

First person to discover Antarctica

The first human to spot Antarctica was believed to be Russian explorer Thaddeus von Bellingshausen, on 27 January 1820. But there are other contenders for this record, including the American seal-hunter, John Davis, in February 1821 and the Norwegian whaler, Henryk Bull, in January 1895.

Largest insect at the poles

The largest insect living inland in Antarctica is in fact tiny! It is a wingless midge, a small fly measuring only 0.5in (12mm). It can be found in the Dry Valleys. Some species of Antarctic fish have evolved natural anti-freeze proteins that allow their blood to remain liquid in sub-freezing temperatures.

World's most famous iceberg

The iceberg that sunk the *Titanic* in April 1912 is probably the most famous of them all. Scientists speculate that the *Titanic*

iceberg may have come from the Jacobshavn glacier located in west Greenland. That glacier is one of the largest on earth (measuring about 9 miles/15km across) and drains most of the Greenland ice sheet. Jacobshavn is also the fastest glacier on Earth, moving over 4.5 miles (7km) in a single year. All of that ice gradually enters the ocean and breaks up into small chunks each year, ranging from 33ft (10m) to 0.62 miles (1km) across.

Largest icebergs in the world

Large icebergs are simply called "bergs," and the largest of all are called "tabular bergs." These are plates of ice that measure up to 3,200ft (1,000m) thick. Some tabular bergs are the size of a small US state. Icebergs come in all different shapes and sizes. "Brash ice" ranges from the size of ice cubes to baseballs. "Bergy bits" refers to icebergs that are larger than baseballs and smaller than beach balls. Icebergs that measure between 3.3ft (1m) and 9.9ft (3m) are called "growlers" because sailors often hear a growling sound as these icebergs bob in the water. "Growlers" are roughly the size of a large piano.

The longest wall

The Great Wall of China stretches over 4,000 miles (6,400km). Designed to help protect China from invasion, its construction started in the 5th century BCE, although some sections were not built until the 16th century.

The longest man-made canal

Engineers have managed to create very important short-cuts for ships

New York's tallest building

When New York's Empire State Building was completed in 1931 it became the world's tallest building, a record it held until 1972 when the World Trade Center was completed. It is 103 floors high, with a total height of 1,454ft (443.2m) including the lightning rod, and it has 6,500 windows. Following the destruction of the World Trade Center, it is still New York's tallest building.

The biggest ancient building

The Great Pyramid of Egypt was the tallest man-made structure on the planet for almost 4,000 years. Located in Giza and completed in 2560BCE, the Great Pyramid took 20 years to build out of huge blocks of stone which were dragged by up to 200,000 workers. The pyramid is the tomb of the Pharaoh Khufu.

300
islands in largest artificial archipelago

Building the world

The ruler of Dubai, Sheikh Mohammed bin Rashid al Maktoum, has created the world's largest artificial group of islands, measuring 5.5 miles (9km) across and called simply "The World." Situated off the coast of Dubai in the Middle East, the ambitious project comprises 300 individual islands, which are grouped together to form a map of the world.

by creating water canals across the land. The longest canal ever built is the ancient Great Canal of China (1,115 miles/1,794km). Some of the most ancient parts of the canal date back to the 5th century BCE. One of the most important is the Panama Canal (51 miles/77km), which was built so that ships could go between the Atlantic and Pacific oceans without having to make the extensive journey around the bottom of South America.

The golden great bridge

When the Golden Gate Bridge in San Francisco, California, USA, was completed in May 1937 it was a truly extraordinary sight. It had the longest suspension span of any bridge in the world. The bridge has a 4,200ft (1,280m) section without any supporting pillars, which is an incredible feat of engineering. It took four years to build and each of its towers is held together with 60,000 rivets. The Akashi-Kaikyo Bridge in Japan, which is also known as Pearl Bridge, now holds the world record for longest suspended span: 6,532ft (1,991m).

The Channel Tunnel

The 31-mile (50-km) long Channel Tunnel is the longest undersea rail tunnel in the world. There had been plans to build a tunnel under the English Channel to link the UK and France since as far back as 1802, but it wasn't until 1994 that the project was finally completed. The Channel Tunnel is actually formed of three separate tunnels bored through chalk 148ft (45m) underneath the English Channel. Every year around 15 million passengers travel between the UK and France through the Tunnel.

Britain's most visited ancient monument

Stonehenge is a circle of huge standing stones in Wiltshire, UK, erected around 2200BCE. At 12ft (4m) tall, the stones weigh up to 28 tons (25,000kg) and some come from 25 miles (40km) away and others may have come from Wales. It has over a million visitors a year, with millions more driving past it.

Skateboarding's toughest move

The 900, a spin that takes you round an incredible two-and-a-half times before coming to land (900 degrees of rotation), is the most difficult move in skateboarding. When Tony Hawk of the USA unveiled it at the 1999 X Games, it took 10 attempts before he could ride out of it – the organizers let him carry on trying and nobody complained – and he won Best Trick by a long margin. Since then it has been mastered by only three others:

World's first ever X Games

The X Games are an annual event aimed at satisfying the rapidly increasing popularity of spectacular action sports – essentially a cool version of the Olympics. Originally named Extreme Games, the first ever X Games event took place in Rhode Island, USA, in July 1995 and was organized by the US TV channel ESPN. It featured BMX, skateboarding, surfing, and Moto X, and when nearly 200,000 people (twice the crowd for a Wembley soccer cup final) turned up, the organizers decided to make it an annual televized event. The Winter X Games were added to ESPN's calendar in January 1997, at Snow Summit Mountain in California. The sports featured were snowboarding, skiing, snowmobiling, and snow skating.

Moto X's most difficult trick

The most challenging move in Moto X is the double back flip, in which the rider comes off the ramp and somersaults through two full rotations before landing their

wheels safely on the deck again. Travis Pastrana of the USA successfully pulled the trick off at the 2006 X Games. Pastrana was awarded the gold medal for Best Trick, and never performed the move again.

Giorgio Zattoni of Italy and Sandro Dias of Brazil in 2004, and Alex Perelson of the USA in 2009.

BMX's most complex move

The no hands 900 is the most demanding move in BMX. After taking off from a vert ramp, the rider performs two-and-a-half rotations without holding on to the handlebars. It was successfully completed by Mat Hoffman of the US at the 2002 X Games but it only won him the silver medal.

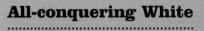

Highest assisted air on a BMX

The record for the highest assisted air is 26.6ft (8.1m) above a 24ft (7.31m) ramp (or approximately 52.5ft/16m off the ground). It was set by Mat Hoffman in 2002, when he was pulled to the ramp by a motorcycle to get the most speed. The highest unassisted air is 19ft (5.79m) above an 18ft (5.48m) ramp (just over 36ft/11m off the ground), set by Dave Mirra of the USA in 2001.

BMX's youngest ever professional

BMX legend Mat Hoffman of the USA was the youngest ever professional in the sport when he relinquished his amateur status at the age of 16. He first competed in BMX at the age of 13. Hoffman is credited with inventing hundreds of now-standard BMX tricks; and is also as famous for his high pain tolerance – he has suffered so many serious injuries during his career that he has had over 20 operations, including one to replace knee ligaments which he underwent without anesthetic.

Highest and longest skateboard jump

In July 2005, Danny Way jumped over the Great Wall of China on a skateboard, setting new records for height (23.5ft/7.16m) and distance (79ft/24.07m) out of a quarter pipe.

All-conquering White

Shaun White is currently the best overall snowboarder in the world, with a total of 10 Winter X Games gold medals for snowboarding (plus two Winter Olympic golds) and one X Games gold for skateboarding. White, famous for his shocking red hair, has been nicknamed "The Flying Tomato." Danny Kass of the USA holds seven Winter X Games

gold medals for snowboarding (and two Winter Olympics medals). Kass's signature move – a backside rodeo – is so difficult it's known as "The Kasseroll."

Most consecutive frontside ollies

An "ollie" is an aerial skateboarding trick invented by Alan Ollie Gelfand, later adapted to flat ground by Rodney Mullen. The record for the most ollies in a row is held by Rob Dyrdek of the US, who performed 46 in 2007 in Los Angeles. The trick is also known as "no hands aerial".

World's tallest Buddha

The Spring Temple Buddha in Henan Province, China, is by far the tallest statue of the Buddha in the world. The Spring Temple Buddha stands 502ft (153m) tall. Planned soon after the blowing up of the Bamiyan Buddhas in Afghanistan, it was completed in 2002.

Most ancient form of Asian medicine

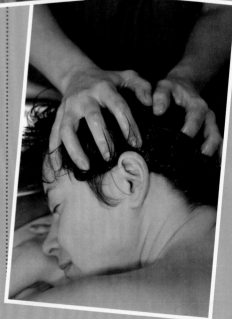

People in India and China had an incredible medical knowledge by the time of the Buddha, which was around 520BCE. Western medicine was a very long way behind. The ancient Indian medical system Ayurveda roughly means "knowledge of life." It was initially passed on orally. The first scripts were inscribed on leaves, then on stone and copper. Still used by millions, the West now draws on its teachings.

The biggest continent

Asia is the world's largest continent, taking up one-third of the total land surface on the planet. It is 17 million sq miles (44 million sq km). Asia also includes almost two-thirds of the world's entire population: 4 billion.

Languages of China

With almost 900 million native speakers, Mandarin has more first language speakers than any other language in the world, even though a lot of Chinese people cannot speak it. If you are in Hong Kong you are more likely to hear Cantonese, or even English, than Mandarin. In all, 90 million people speak Wu, 60 million speak Min, and 80 million speak Cantonese.

Population records

China is the world's most densely populated country. Almost 1.4 billion people live there, most in cities like Beijing. India is the second-largest country, with 1.1 billion people. The UN Population Division has projected the world population – now just over 6.8 billion – will surpass 9 billion by 2050.

Giants of Japanese industry

Japan has the second largest economy in the world, with an annual gross domestic product (GDP) of $5 trillion. The Japanese are known for their efficiency and hard work. China, close behind, has a GDP of $4.9 trillion, while India has a GDP of $1.2 trillion. China and India are now advancing rapidly and they are predicted to be, in a few years time, the most economically powerful countries in Asia. In terms of GDP by purchasing power parity, China has the largest economy in Asia and the second largest in the world.

700
million bicycles in China

The strangest Japanese inventions

Japan has become known as a nation of inventors. It is particularly famous for inventing technologically advanced electronic gadgets, such as the digital watch, but it is also known for some of the weirdest inventions of all time. These include: a bath body suit which allows you to have a bath without getting wet; headgear that can dispense tissues; and a hair-guard to protect you from being splashed by noodles!

The world's most literate warriors

The samurai of Japan are regarded as the most literate warriors in history. They had a set of values derived from Buddhism, Confucianism, and Shintoism. Their ethical code spread across the realm as they idealized the arts, specializing in them. From the earliest Japanese writings such as the Kojiki, the samurai were expected to be cultured and literate. Bun Bu Ryo Do – "the pen and the sword in accord" – was the ideal most aspired to. The Katana, a curved saber sword, was regarded as the soul of the samurai – they even gave their swords names. The samurai were fierce in battle, but were bound by a rigorous code of honor. If they offended this code, or were defeated in battle, they would take their own lives.

Most bikes in the world

China holds the record for being the country with the most bicycles in the world, with about 700 million people choosing to travel through the crowded Chinese cities on two wheels, some of them electric.

The tiny monster

The smallest dinosaur may have been a two-legged theropod which was no bigger than a turkey. The Compsognathus, whose name means "elegant jaw," was about 3ft (1m) long and weighed about 6.5lb (2.5kg). Its eyes were large in proportion to the rest of its skull. The Compsognathus lived in Europe

Greatest creatures on earth

The term dinosaur, coined in 1842 by the English biologist Sir Richard Owen, is derived from the Greek words "deinos" (terrible, stiff, masterly, skilful) and "sauros" (lizard). Dinosaurs were reptiles, and were the dominant vertebrates of terrestrial ecosystems for over 160 million years. They lived from the Late Triassic period 220–230 million years ago and through the Jurassic and Cretaceous periods, until they became extinct about 65 million years ago. There are two groups of dinosaurs. The ornithischians and the saurischians. The ornithischians had bird-like hips and beaks and they were herbivores, eating only plants. The saurischians were split into two types: the big, four-legged herbivores called sauropods, such as the Apatosaurus (formerly known as Brontosaurus), and the two-legged predators called theropods, such as the Tyrannosaurus rex and Velociraptor.

The biggest of them all

The biggest dinosaurs to roam the Earth are now thought to be the titanosaurs, which included the Bruhathkayosaurus and the Argentinasaurus. They were sauropod herbivores that may have weighed more than 110 tons (100,000kg). They flourished in the Late Cretaceous period. Previously, the biggest dinosaur was thought to be the Brachiosaurus.

in the Late Jurassic period, around 150 million years ago, and it fed on small lizards. The remains of even smaller dinosaurs have been found since, but scientists continue to argue about the validity of these specimens.

Speedy ostrich

The fastest dinosaur to have existed on planet Earth was an ornithomimid (a bird-like theropod), such as the Dromiceiomimus or the Gallimimus. The Gallimimus, which lived in the Gobi Desert in the Late Cretaceous period, bears a slight resemblance to the modern-day ostrich. It walked on two long legs and had a long beak-like snout and a long neck. By examining its track marks fossilized in mud, scientists have deduced that it may have run at a speed of over 30mph (48kph).

The fiercest dinosaur

The fiercest, most aggressive dinosaur was the Velociraptor, but as it only grew to be about 6ft (2m) long, it would have been no match for the Tyrannosaurus rex. The name of this dinosaur means "tyrant lizard king" and it was one of the biggest predators to live on land. It was 43ft (13m) long and weighed 7.5 tons (68,000kg). The T.rex had huge pointy teeth, which could rip anything to shreds.

The armor-plated dinosaur

The Ankylosaurid was the most heavily armored dinosaur that protected itself from predators, with a record-breaking array of defensive weapons. It had a thick layer of armor consisting of overlapping plates of leathery skin, rows of spikes along its body and a tail shaped like a club. Some Ankylosaurids even had armor-plated eyelids!

The biggest claw

The Deinocheirus, which roamed the Earth in the Late Cretaceous period, has the largest, most fearsome claws of all dinosaurs. It was a saurischian carnivore and one of the most deadly theropods known. Fossil finds in the Gobi Desert, Mongolia, in 1965 revealed a creature with arms that were 8ft (2.4m) long. Each arm had three fingers with long, hook-like claws, 8–12in (20–30cm) long. The Deinocheirus' hands alone measured 2ft (60 cm).

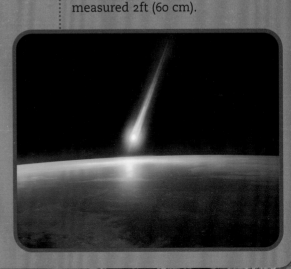

The world's first steam engine

A rotary turbine invented in Egypt in the 16th century by Taqi al-Din was the world's first steam engine. Hundred years later, the first steam engine with industrial capabilities was invented by Jeronimo de Ayanz y Beumont of Spain. Scotsman James Watt, in the 18th century, applied the theories to supply rotary

The big bang theory

Because gunpowder had been invented in China as far back as the 9th century, the cannon had long-since replaced battering rams and siege engines as a battlefield necessity by the time it came to Europe, courtesy of Spain's Moorish invaders in the 1200s. According to records, those Islamic armies also had handguns.

The earliest steel production

Steel is iron, alloyed with a percentage of carbon. This percentage is 0.2 and 1.7, depending on the grade – the greater the carbon content the higher the grade. Although there is evidence that steel was produced as far back as Ancient China and India, it wasn't until the 1850s that Henry Bessemer invented an inexpensive production method and steel began to be used widely in the construction industry and for shipbuilding and railway building.

The first printing press

The first printing presses were made from modified grape or olive presses, allowing the printed word to go into mass production all over Europe. The invention of the moveable type printing press is seen

1810
the year Peter Durant invented the tin can

power – which was controllable with gears, for use in factories. His vital changes to steam engine design made them more efficient and cheaper to run. Such easily available, on-site power was one of the main facilitators of the British Industrial Revolution.

as having had as great an impact on Medieval society as the Internet did on this century. Gutenberg, who invented the printing press in 1436, also developed a lead and tin alloy to make easily handled, long-lasting letters, and used an oil-based ink. His technology was a key factor in the European Renaissance.

Skyscraping technology

Without steel, the famous New York City skyline would look very different from the way it does today – the Empire State Building is the most famous steel-framed building in the world. In the 1920s and 1930s, once buildings started to be constructed on steel frames, they were able to rise much higher much more quickly, and more cost-effectively. Skyscraper towers soon began to dominate the major cities across the globe.

The first filaments

Thomas Edison is well-known for having invented the long-lasting filament, which turned the light bulb into a widely accessible invention in the 1880s. However, several different people had been developing the filament during the previous 80 years. Humphrey Davy invented the platinum filament in 1802; Warren de la Rue invented the vacuum enclosure in 1840; and Joseph Swan invented the carbon fiber filament in 1873.

Can this be true?

The can was invented in 1810 by Englishman Peter Durand as a method of keeping food fresh in a tin-lined iron vessel. His invention made a huge impact on food preservation. In 1813, the first commercial canning factory opened in England. The first cans were so thick they had to be opened with a hammer and chisel. These days, tin cans will have virtually no tin in their composition; they used to be made of rolled steel coated with tin, but, since the 1960s, they have been made almost exclusively out of aluminum.

Most World Cup wins

Brazil are soccer legends, having won the World Cup five times – 1958, 1962, 1970, 1994, and 2002 – which is more than any other nation. They have appeared in seven World Cup finals, and are the only nation to have competed in every one of the 18 World Cup competitions since it began in 1930.

Most World Cup goals

The record goalscorer in the history of the World Cup is the Brazilian, Ronaldo Luis Nazário de Lima, who found the net 15 times over three competitions, in 1998, 2002, and 2006).

Youngest World Cup player

Norman Whiteside was the youngest to appear in a World Cup, debuting for N. Ireland at 17 years, 41 days, at Espana 82. However, Pelé, born Edson Arantes do Nascimento, was just 17 years and 8 months in the 1958 competition – his goal in the quarter-final against Wales makes him the youngest-ever goalscorer in the World Cup. He went on to score a hat-trick in the semi-final against France, and two further goals in the final against the host nation, Sweden. Pelé is universally accepted as the greatest soccer player of all time.

Oldest World Cup player

This honor goes to Roger Milla of Cameroon, who was 42 years and 39 days when he played in the 1994 World Cup. Milla, who was famous for his celebrations, dances and wide grin, managed to score in the match against Russia, despite his advancing years.

Youngest England International

Theo Walcott became the youngest player in an England shirt, making his International debut against Hungary on 30 May 2006, at 17 years 75 days. Following in the "youngest" list are Wayne Rooney, who first played for England aged 17 years 111 days, and Michael Owen, the sixth youngest, at 18 years 60 days.

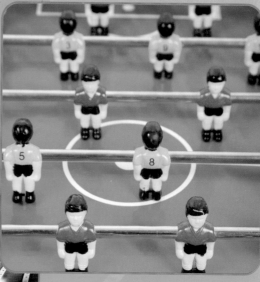

The best in Europe

Germany has won the European Cup three times: in 1972, 1980, and 1996. They have also been runners-up twice, making them the most successful soccer side in Europe, followed by France, with two wins.

Quickest ever World Cup goal

There have been some very quick ones, but nothing beats Hakan Sükür's goal against Korea at the 2002 World Cup. The Turkish striker managed to get the ball in the net just 11 seconds after kick-off!

The most FA Cup wins

This record is held by Manchester United, who have lifted the FA trophy 11 times (1909, 1948, 1963, 1977, 1983, 1985, 1990, 1994, 1996, 1999, and 2004).

Goalkeeping records

Gordon Banks's fingertip save for England against Pelé in the 1970 World Cup is acknowledged by many people to be the greatest save of all time. From what looked like an impossible position, Banks dived the full width of the goal and managed to tip the ball over the bar. Italy's Gianluigi Buffon is regarded as the best modern-day goalkeeper and the most expensive – he cost Juventus $82 million (£41 million) when they bought him from Parma.

Referee records

Juan Gardeazábal of Spain is the youngest-ever World Cup referee at 24 years and 193 days. Joel Quiniou of France has refereed most matches: eight times between 1986 and 1994.

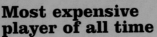

Most expensive player of all time

This record is held by Portugal's Cristiano Ronaldo when he transferred from Manchester United to Real Madrid in 2009 for an amazing $132 million (£80 million). In 2008, when Manchester United won the UEFA Champions League, the Portuguese genius was named both 'Player of the Tournament' and FIFA World Player of the Year.

World Cup bad boys

Giampiero Marini of Italy holds the distinction of getting the fastest ever caution. He was shown the yellow card during the first minute of Italy's World Cup game against Poland in 1982. Fastest ever sending off goes to José Batista of Uruguay, who was sent off after 56 seconds against Scotland in the 1986 World Cup. Joint record-holders for the most cards (red or yellow) in a World Cup game are France's Zinedine Zidane and Brazil's Cafu, who have both been dismissed six times.

Five!

The five senses that human beings have are: hearing, sight, taste, smell, and touch.

Help with hearing

Henry Fletcher invented the first hearing aid while he worked at Bell Laboratories in the US in the early 20th century. The human ear is fully developed at birth, but most people experience some loss of hearing as they get older. Today's hearing aids are sophisticated and advanced gadgets. You can hardly tell when someone is wearing one.

Balancing tricks

Balance, or equilibrium, depends on information that is sent to your brain primarily from our hearing, but also from our visual and muscle feedback. The sensory organs in the inner ear enable you to balance and do things like walk along a narrow plank without falling off. Some people, such as tightrope walkers, can perform incredible feats of balance. The world's longest tightrope was constructed in Seoul, South Korea, on 4 May 2007. The rope stretched 0.6 miles (1km) across the Han River. China's Abudusataer Wujiabudula successfully walked the rope in just 11min 22.49sec, a new world record. Jorge Ojeda-Guzman of Florida, USA, holds the record for the longest time on a tightrope. He stayed up there from 1 January to 25 June – a total of 205 days.

205
days spent on a tightrope

Smelly records

Taste is the ability to detect flavor in food or poison. There are five basic tastes: bitter, salty, sour, sweet, or fermented. Smell is the ability of the nose to perceive odors or scents. The two work together: 70–75% of what we think is taste actually comes from our sense of smell. The smelliest town on Earth is Rotorua, New Zealand. It's built in a volcanic thermal area, which means there are lots of geysers and hot springs, as well as a fairly unpleasant odor.

Nicknamed "Sulphur City," the town wreaks of old rotten eggs. In 2004, the stinkiest cheese was found to be Vieux-Boulogne, a French cow's milk cheese. During production, the cheese is washed in beer. In 2007, it was reaffirmed that it was still the world's smelliest cheese.

The first 3-D film

In the late 1890s, William Friese-Greene patented the first 3-D movie process. A half-century later, in 1952, *Bwana Devil* was the first color, American 3-D feature. It was about the Tsavo man-eating lions and started a 3-D boom in the US film industry. 3-D stands for three dimensional – referring to the length, width, and height of our physical surroundings.

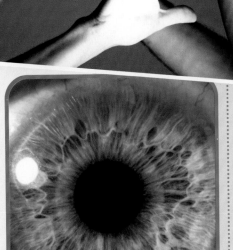

Seeing with your fingers

Touch is the ability to sense pressure on the skin. Human sense of touch is amazingly acute – we can feel something as small as a tiny dot on our fingertips. In 1821, blind people were able to read and write by using touch for the first time, when Louis Braille invented the Braille system.

Darkest, lightest

The darkest place on Earth is Lake Vostok, the largest of over 140 subglacial lakes under Antarctica. It has more oxygen than any other lake on Earth. Yuma, Arizona, USA, is the sunniest place on Earth. Out of a possible 4,456 hours of daylight per year, Yuma gets 4,050. That means it's sunny 90% of the time.

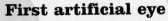

First artificial eye

In 1579, the Venetians invented the first artificial eye. These were thin shells of glass with sharp edges. The wearers had to remove the eyes at night to get relief from discomfort and to avoid breakage. Technology did not advance much until the 1800s, when German glassblower Ludwig Muller-Uri, who made life-like eyes for dolls, developed a glass eye for his son.

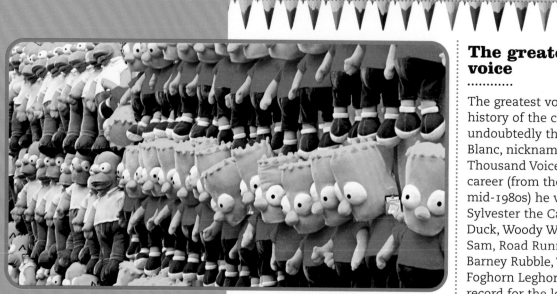

The greatest cartoon voice

The greatest vocal artist in the history of the cartoon is undoubtedly the American Mel Blanc, nicknamed "The Man of a Thousand Voices." In a 50-year-long career (from the mid-1930s to the mid-1980s) he voiced Bugs Bunny, Sylvester the Cat, Porky Pig, Daffy Duck, Woody Woodpecker, Yosemite Sam, Road Runner, Elmer Fudd, Taz, Barney Rubble, Tweety Bird, and Foghorn Leghorn. Blanc holds the record for the longest time any animated character has been performed by his or her original voice contributor (for his characterization of Daffy Duck, which lasted over 52 years).

Brilliant Bugs

The American TV magazine *TV Guide* named Walt Disney's Bugs Bunny the best cartoon character of all time in its 50th Anniversary issue. Bugs was "born" in 1938.

The most episodes of a cartoon series

This record goes to the Japanese animé series *Sazae-San*, which has over 6,000 episodes to its credit.

6,000
record-breaking run of Sazae-San

However, *The Simpsons*, which celebrated 20 years on the air in 2009, has notched up 459 episodes as of April 2010. Although Homer, Bart, and company were briefly overtaken when *Scooby-Doo* entered its third rebirth and reached 371, *The Simpsons* passed the magic 400 mark in 2007. *The Simpsons* was first broadcast in December 1989 and is going strong today. This makes it the longest-running TV sitcom in the world, whether live action or animated.

The longest-running television cartoon

This honor goes to the Japanese animé series *Sazae-San*, which has run from 1969 to the present day. However, *Scooby-Doo* holds the honor for a non-animé cartoon after it also made its debut in 1969 and its final episode was aired in 2005. However, the dog-turned-detective needed three different incarnations to set this record: the original *Scooby-Doo* ran from 1969 to 1985; A

Pup Named Scooby-Doo ran from 1988 until 1991, and *What's New Scooby-Doo?* launched in 2002 to run for three years.

Once upon a time in Springfield

The Simpsons started out as a short regular item on *The Tracey Ullman Show* in 1989, and while that sketch series is long forgotten, Homer, Bart, and co have gone on to win all sorts of records. It was voted The Best Television Show of the Century by *Time* magazine; Bart was the only fictional character included in the 100 Most Influential Americans; and in the UK it was voted Channel 4's top Children's Show and Top TV Cartoon. It is also a multi-billion

dollar industry, with merchandizing ranging from toothpaste to board games. The single "Do The Bartman" topped the UK charts for 3 weeks.

Walt Disney's most famous creation

The most popular cartoon character in the world is Mickey Mouse – he is so well-known that you only need to see the ears! Walt Disney created

Mickey in 1928. For Walt, who had started Walt Disney Productions with his brother Roy in the garage of their uncle's house, Mickey represented their big breakthrough, and, by the 1930s, Mickey Mouse had eclipsed Felix the Cat as America's most popular cartoon. Donald Duck, Goofy, and a series of full-length animated features followed, making the The Walt Disney Company one of the most profitable studios in the world.

Deep Earth

The deepest part of the Earth (at 1,512 miles/2,433km deep) is a solid that contains both iron and nickel. It is because of this that the center of the earth is a magnet, like a compass. It generates a magnetic field that protects the earth from flying out of orbit.

Rocky sticky molten mantle

The Russian Kola borehole SG-3 remains the deepest ever drilled into the earth's crust. It reached 40,230ft (12,100m) in 1989, a third of the way through the Baltic crust, touching 2.5 billion-year-old rocks. The longest hole, the 40,320ft (12,200m) Maersk Oil hole in Qatar, is primarily horizontal. The Earth's 1,800-mile (2,900-km) thick mantle is rocky, sticky, and molten – like a solid plastic. The mantle makes up 70 per cent of the Earth.

Cores – inner and outer

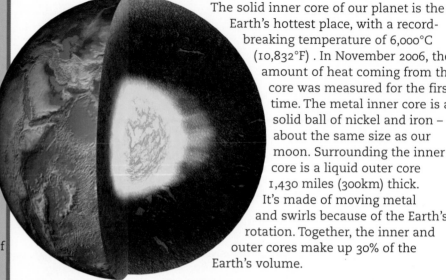

The solid inner core of our planet is the Earth's hottest place, with a record-breaking temperature of 6,000°C (10,832°F) . In November 2006, the amount of heat coming from the core was measured for the first time. The metal inner core is a solid ball of nickel and iron – about the same size as our moon. Surrounding the inner core is a liquid outer core 1,430 miles (300km) thick. It's made of moving metal and swirls because of the Earth's rotation. Together, the inner and outer cores make up 30% of the Earth's volume.

Earth's crust

The Earth has the most complex crust of the planets in our solar system. The crust accounts for less than 1 per cent of the Earth's volume and is extremely thin in comparison to the other three layers (the inner core, outer core, and mantle). There are two types of crust: the oceanic crust and the continental crust. The crust is only about 3–5 miles (8km) thick under the oceans (oceanic crust) and 25 miles (32km) thick under the continents (continental crust). The temperatures of the crust vary from air temperature on the surface to about 870°C (1,600°F) in the deepest parts of the crust. The crust of the Earth is broken into pieces called "plates" that float on the soft mantle that is located below the crust – when these plates stick, and pressure builds up, it results in an earthquake.

Clarke's discovery

Frank Wigglesworth Clarke was the first to discover the composition of the Earth's crust. Wigglesworth, an American chemist known as the "Father of Geochemistry," found that

47 per cent of the crust is oxygen. The mineral Clarkeite, a uranium oxide, was named after him. One-twelfth of the Earth's crust is made from aluminum, although it exists there only as a compound. In 1886, US college student Charles Martin Hall discovered an inexpensive way to produce pure aluminum. His discovery caused the price of aluminum to fall from $20/kg (£13/kg) to less than $1/kg (£0.65/kg)!

Amazing atmosphere

The Earth's atmosphere is an envelope of gases surrounding the Earth, and held down by gravity. It is divided into five different layers, the troposphere being the closest to Earth, and the Exosphere being the most distant (at 6,213 miles/ 10,000km). At an altitude of 328,000ft (100km), the atmosphere becomes outer space at the Kármán line, a fact first calculated by the Hungarian-American engineer and physicist Theodore von Kármán.

Longest journey to the center?

Ecuador's Mount Chimborazo is the point on Earth furthest from the core. If you were to travel from the core to the top of Chimborazo you would journey through a record-breaking 3,728 miles (6,384.4km). A dormant volcano last active in the first millennium AD, the top of Chimborazo is covered by glaciers. The first climbers to scale it were Edward Whymper and Louis and Jean-Antoine Carrel in 1880.

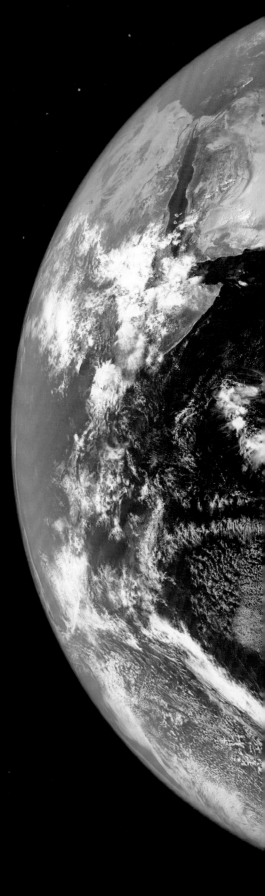

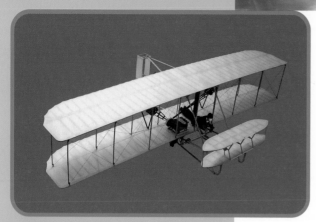

Flight of the Wright brothers

The Wright brothers, Orville (1871–1948) and Wilbur (1867–1912), made the first successful air flight on 17 December 1903 in *Kitty Hawk*, North Carolina, USA. The first flight only went 120ft (36.5m) and lasted 12 seconds, but they had proved that human flight was possible.

Adventures of Steve Fossett

In 2005, the American adventurer Steve Fossett (1944–2007) became the first person ever to fly a plane around the world solo, non-stop, without refuelling. Fossett flew from Salina, Kansas, in his plane, the *Virgin Atlantic Global Flyer*. He landed back at Salina 67 hours later. He was also the first man to fly solo, non-stop, around the world in a balloon, and was a skilled sailor and cross-country skier. Fossett went missing when his plane disappeared without trace in Nevada, USA, on 3 September 2007.

Jumbo jets

The first jumbo jet was the Boeing 747, which has been flown commercially from 1970. Inside, it is a double-decker, which can seat 524 passengers. It held the world record for the most passengers on an aircraft until the Airbus A380 made its first commercial flight in 2007. The A380 can hold up to 853 people.

Fastest jet plane

Apart from prototypes and unmanned rocket planes, the fastest jet plane in operation is the Lockheed SR-71, known as the *Blackbird*, which can exceed speeds of Mach 3.2. That is 3.2 times the speed of sound, or 2,464mph

171
days to fly around the world in a helicopter

Solo across the Atlantic

Spirit of St Louis, a monoplane piloted by Charles Lindbergh, made the first solo transatlantic flight between the American and the European mainland on 20 May 1907. The plane flew from New York to Paris in 33hr 30min. Amelia Earhart became the first woman to fly solo across the Atlantic on the same date in 1932.

Most advanced bomber

The B-2 *Spirit* stealth bomber is the most advanced bomber in military service. It is virtually invisible to radar as it is made from secret materials and coatings. It can reach almost supersonic speeds despite the fact that it carries a lot of heavy bombs and it has an un-refuelled range of 6,000 miles (9,600km).

(3,952kph). The fastest unmanned jet-powered aircraft is NASA's *X-43A* scramjet, which reaches a speed of Mach 9.6 – nearly 7,000mph (11,265kph).

Flight endurance record

The longest non-stop passenger flight on record was TWA's first ever flight between London and San Francisco in October 1957. The plane, a Lockheed *Constellation*, took 23hr 19mins to travel 5,357 miles (8,621 km). Today, a non-stop journey from London to San Francisco takes about 11 hours.

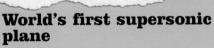

Pole-to-pole helicopter ride

In 2007, a 67-year-old grandmother broke the record for flying around the world via the North and South Poles in a helicopter. Americans Jennifer Murray (b. 1940) and co-pilot Colin Bodill (b. 1952) completed the 32,000 mile (51,500km) journey in 171 days. They made 101 refuelling stops in their Bell helicopter. In their previous attempt in 2003, they crash-landed in a near-fatal accident in the Antarctic. Murray became the first solo woman to circumnavigate the globe in a helicopter in 1997.

World's first supersonic plane

Concorde became the first ever supersonic passenger plane when it took to the skies for its first scheduled flight on 21 March 1976. Supersonic means "faster than the speed of sound." *Concorde*'s average cruising speed was 1,330mph (2,140kph) and it could cross the Atlantic in 3h 30min, which was twice as fast as any other passenger plane.

400 meters hurdles

Californian Kevin Young holds the world record for the 400m hurdles, with a time of 46.78sec, run at the Barcelona Olympics in 1992. This record was all the more remarkable because Young failed to clear the last hurdle cleanly, grazing it and stumbling slightly. He is also the only 400m hurdler to have run under 47 seconds. The women's record is held by Yuliya Pechonkina, who ran 52.34sec in Tula, Russia, in 2003.

110 meters hurdles

The men's world record for 110m hurdles is held by Cuba's Dayron Robles and it was run in Ostrava, in the Czech Republic on 12 June 2008 in 12.87 secs. The women's record was set by Bulgarian Yordanka Donkova in 1998, at 12.21sec.

Ten events in one

The decathlon is considered to be the greatest test of an individual's athletic prowess, as it combines running, jumping, and throwing to make ten separate events. The full list of decathlon events is: 100m; 400m; 1500m; long jump; shot put; high jump; 110m hurdles; discus; pole vault; and javelin. The events usually take place over two days and competitors are awarded points for how well they perform in each discipline. The winner is the athlete with the greatest total.

Men's decathlon

The decathlon world record for men is held by Roman Sebrle from the Czech Republic, who scored 9,026 at a meet in Götzis, Austria, on 27 May 2001. His achievements in each event were: 100m, 10.64sec; long jump, 8.1m; shot put, 15.33m; high jump, 2.12m; 400m, 47.79sec; 110m hurdles, 13.92sec; discus, 47.92m; pole vault, 4.80m; javelin, 70.16m; 1500m, 4min21.98sec.

Women's decathlon

The record-holder is Lithuanian Austra Skujyte, who scored 8,366 points in Columbia, USA, on 15 April 2005. Her scores were: 100m, 12.49sec; long jump, 6.12m; shot put, 16.42m; high jump, 1.78m; 400m, 57.19sec; 100m hurdles, 14.22sec; discus, 46.19m; pole vault, 3.10m; javelin, 48.78m; 1500m, 5min15.86sec. The women's decathlon is still not an Olympic discipline.

First female pole vault

At the 2000 Olympics in Sydney, Australia, the women's pole vault was accepted as an Olympic event for the first time. Stacy Dragila won the gold medal, to become the first ever champion in the event. The current undisputed queen of the pole vault is Yelena Isinbayeva, who holds the world record at 5.06m.

The greatest heptathlete

The Heptathlon consists of seven disciplines – 100m and 400m, high jump, shot put, long jump, javelin, and 800m – and is a women-only event. The current world record-holder is Jackie Joyner-Kersee, who scored 7,291 points at Seoul, South Korea, on 24 September 1988. Her times and distances were as follows: 100m, 12,49sec; high jump, 1,78m; shot put, 15.80m; 200m, 22.56sec; long jump, 7.27m; javelin, 45.66m; 800m, 2min8.51sec. Jackie is the sister of Olympic triple jump champion Al Joyner and the sister-in-law of Florence Griffith-Joyner. She is one of the greatest female athletes of all time, having won three Olympic golds for heptathlon (1988 and 1992) and long jump (1988) and four World Championship golds (1987 long jump and heptathlon; 1991 long jump; 1993 heptathlon). She also played basketball for UCLA and has been honored as one of their 15 greatest-ever players.

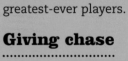

Giving chase

Salf Saaeed Shaheen of Qatar (formerly Stephen Cherono of Kenya) holds the record for the men's 3000m steeplechase at 7min 53.63sec (set in Brussels in 2004). Russian Guinara Samitova is the women's world record-holder, with a time of 8min 58.81sec (set in Beijing in 2008).

The earliest cities

The Mesopotamians, an ancient civilization situated in modern-day Iraq, were the first people to really establish city life. The Mesopotamian village of Eridu, 200 miles (320km) south of Baghdad, was founded in about 5400BCE and, over the centuries, grew into being a city with important temples and a range of

dwellings made from mud-bricks and reeds. Cities were also formed in Central America and the Indus Valley in Asia before any developed in Europe.

The first million-person city

Cities of over one million people are now common all over the world, but the very first is believed to have been Baghdad in Iraq. By the 8th century, it had a population of over one million. People moved there because it was a good place for

trade. But, as accurate censuses did not take place before the 18th century, some argue that Rome had a population of one million by the 1st century.

The fastest-growing city

Dubai is the fastest-growing city in the world. Its population increased from 265,000 in 1980 to over 1.3 million in 2006. Situated in the United Arab Emirates, Dubai is undertaking some of the hugest building projects in the world,

constructing the tallest skyscrapers, the biggest man-made islands, and thousands of residential buildings. Three hundred new hotels are currently being built there.

Densest population

The densest city in the world, which means the city with most people living in each square mile, is Mumbai in India. It has almost 78,000 people per sq mile (30,000 people per sq km). Kolkata, also in India, is the second densest city, with 62,000 people per sq mile (29,300 people per sq km).

The state inside a city

The Vatican City in Italy, home of the Pope, is the only state that is contained entirely within a city (Rome). The tiny sovereign state covers 0.2 sq miles (0.5 sq km). It has a population of 770, none of whom are permanent residents. The Vatican City is the spiritual home for the world's Roman Catholics, and is also known as the Holy See.

The abandoned city

Some cities, towns, and villages have become entirely abandoned, usually due to a disaster or because transport networks are changed. The biggest modern city to be abandoned is Prypiat in the Ukraine. Its population of 50,000 left in 1986 due to the Chernobyl nuclear disaster, which made it too dangerous to live there.

Biggest cities in the world

Shanghai in China has the largest city population in the world, with 19 million, followed by Mumbai with 14 million. Karachi in Pakistan is the third largest (12.9 million), before Delhi (12.5 million). If you include the metropolitan area around a city, Tokyo in Japan is the biggest, with over 35 million people. That's over three times the population of Greece.

The safest and most violent places to live

According to US government figures, the most violent place to live in the US is Detroit, Michigan. It is the city with the highest reported gun crime and incidents of

violence. The city was founded by Antoine de la Mothe Cadillac on 24 July 1701, and is the center of the car manufacturing industry in the US. Figures from the same government body say that the safest place to live in the USA is Minneapolis, in Minnesota.

The most visited city

In 2009, Paris became the most visited city in the world, welcoming over 17 million travelers, as London slipped to second place, with 15 million. Bangkok came third (11 million), followed by Singapore at 10 million. New York City, the most visited city in the USA, replaced Las Vegas, known to have sold 40 million hotel rooms in 2007.

Snake racing to extinction

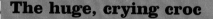

The Alsophis antiguae, known as the Antiguan racer, is the rarest snake in the world. It only lives on Great Bird Island near Antigua and was believed to be extinct until it was rediscovered in 1989. Despite conservation attempts, there are probably only 60–80 adults remaining. They are about 3ft (1m) long. Unusually for a snake, the females are much bigger than the males.

The huge, crying croc

Saltwater crocodiles from Southeast Asia and Australia are the biggest of all reptiles. The longest crocodile ever measured top-to-tail was the skin of a deceased crocodile, which was 20.3ft (6.2m) long. But since skins shrink after removal from the carcass, this crocodile's living length was estimated at 27ft (8.22m). Saltwater crocodiles cry after they have consumed their victims – but only to get rid of the excess salt.

The poisonous lizards

The Gila monster and the Mexican beaded lizard look very similar, with bead-like scales on their backs, and both live in the south of North America.

They are also the only two venomous lizards in the world. They bite their victims and hold on for as long as possible to allow the venom to seep into the wound.

The color-changing chameleons

Madagascar, an island off the east coast of Africa, boasts both the biggest and the smallest chameleons. The parson's chameleon can be 24in (60cm) long while the pygmy stump-tailed ones are just 1.4in (3.5cm). All 160 chameleon species are able to change their skin color. They are camouflaged to match their surroundings, but recent research has shown that they also use their color changes to communicate and to attract a mate.

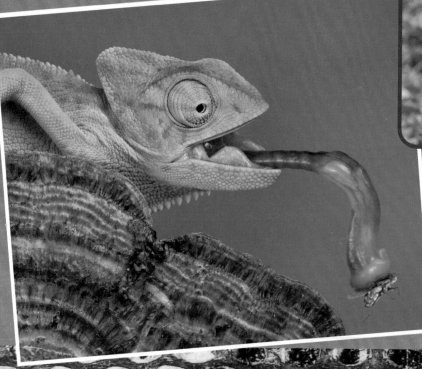

The oldest reptile

The turtle is the oldest living reptile and has a longer average lifespan than the human being. One turtle, a giant tortoise called Addwaitya, was a resident of Kolkata zoo in India and was said to have been the pet of Robert Clive of India in the mid-18th century. It did not die until 2006, making it over 250 years old.

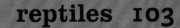

250
age of the oldest turtle

As quick as lightning

Reptiles don't usually move quickly, but the spiny-tailed iguana (Ctenosaura similes) from Costa Rica holds the world sprint record for lizards. It reached a speed of 21mph (34kph) at the research lab of the University of Wisconsin, USA, in 1998.

The fastest snake

Snakes look as if they move faster than they are because of their side to side motion. The fastest snake is the black mamba, but it only travels at 10mph (16kph).

The oldest alligator

Alligators usually live to be about 50 years old, but Muja, who has lived in Belgrade Zoo in Serbia since 1937, is over 73. Alligators look very similar to crocodiles but have wider, shorter heads, with darker bodies. They rarely grow to over 13ft (4m). There are two types: the American alligator and the much rarer and smaller Chinese one. There are only about 200 Chinese alligators in existence.

The toxic newt

Newts are kept as pets but they can be poisonous. The rough-skinned newt from North America is the most poisonous of all, releasing powerful toxins through its skin to put off predators. Humans can die from the poison if they swallow a whole one. The US state of Oregon has recorded the highest instance of "death by newt" in the world.

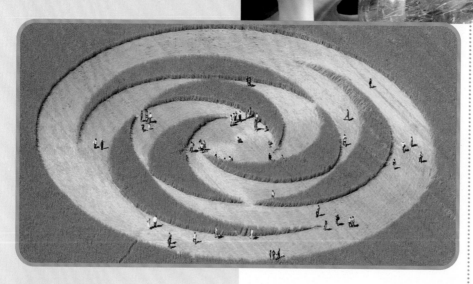

Telepathy

The term "telepathy" was first coined by F.W.H. Myers in 1882 from the Greek words tele, meaning distant, and pathe, meaning feeling. It means being able to transfer thoughts from one mind to another and so communicate while giving no external indications, or to be able to influence how others think. Although there is no firm evidence that telepathy among humans has ever existed, it's a sci-fi and superhero favorite – the Jedi in *Star Wars*, and *Star Trek*'s Vulcans were all telepathic.

Chinese board games

The first Ouija board was used in China in 1200BCE.

Crop circles: real or hoaxes?

Where and when the earliest crop circle occurred is unclear. Some say it was in 1678 in an incident called the "Mowing of the Devil". The legend goes that a farmer's field was visited by an entity that trampled the crops down in a circle. Others believe crop circles go back to biblical times. Crop circles have been appearing around the world with increasing frequency for the last 25 years, and continue to baffle just about everybody. The perfect form of the crop circles can only be fully appreciated from high above ground level, so whoever (or whatever) directed their creation would have needed to be hovering over them. And there is never any evidence of human involvement.

Prison sightings

The Eastern State Penitentiary in Philadelphia, USA, which in 1929 held America's best-known gangster Al Capone on charges of illegal weapons possession, is haunted by former inmates. Built for 250 inmates, at its height it held 1,700. Sightings have been reported in cellblocks 4, 6, and 12.

17

ghosts in the most haunted house

Most famous ghost tale

Charles Dickens's *A Christmas Carol* is the most well-known ghost story. In it, Ebenezer Scrooge is shown the error of his penny-pinching ways by the three ghosts of Christmas Past, Christmas Present, and Christmas Yet To Come.

Most famous ghost photo

Raynham Hall, in Norfolk, UK, which dates back to the 17th century, is said to be haunted by the "Brown Lady." In September 1936, Captain Provand and Indre Shira, two photographers from *Country Life* magazine visiting the property, captured a strange luminous shape descending the main staircase. The photograph is probably the most famous picture of a ghost ever taken.

The paranormal on film

When a human being or inanimate object becomes an instrument to be used by a paranormal force, we say they are "possessed". This is also a popular film-plot device. Possession is usually ended with an exorcism, as in the Hollywood film *The Exorcist* which, to date, has grossed over $440,000,000 (£286,000,000) worldwide.

Britain's most haunted house

This record goes to the fantastic gothic ruins at Alton Towers in Staffordshire, which has no fewer than 17 ghosts in attendance.

Britain's historic homes are full of ghosts and spirits, and the most haunted National Trust home is Blickling Hall in Norfolk, where the headless apparition of Henry VIII's second wife, Anne Boleyn, regularly appears to visitors and staff, with her head held in her lap.

The White House ghosts

The most-seen ghost in the White House (where the US President lives and works) is that of Abraham Lincoln, who became 16th president of the US on 6 November 1860. There have been hundreds of sightings, many of which have come from reliable sources, such as Grace Coolidge, who was the wife of the 30th president of the US, Calvin Coolidge, and Queen Wilhelmina of the Netherlands, who spotted the ex-president when she was a guest of the White House. It is said that Lincoln had a dream in which he saw people surrounding his own dead body in the East Room at the White House, so anticipating his death at the hands of John Wilkes Booth in 1865.

Karate

Karate is the most widely practiced of all the Oriental martial arts, and there are more than 70 different styles. It began in Okinawa in the 17th century. The most popular Japanese styles are Shotokan, Wado Ryu, Goju Ryu, and Shito Ryu.

Tae kwon do

Tae kwon do became an official medal event for the first time at the 2000 Sydney Olympic Games. During those Games, 103 athletes – 55 men and 48 women – from 51 countries took part in the competition. It is one of only two Asian martial arts (judo being the other) in the Olympic Games program.

Judo

In 2004, Ryoko Tamura successfully defended the Olympic title she had

Bruce Lee style

Martial arts film stars Bruce Lee, Jackie Chan, and Jet Li all practiced various styles of kung fu, but Bruce Lee studied many other styles of fighting – including Western boxing – to devise his own very attacking style he called Jute Keen Do, "way of the intercepting fist".

won in 2000. She therefore became the first judoka (a judo practitioner) to retain her Olympic title.

Sumo wrestling

The heaviest sumo wrestler in history was Konishike. Born in Hawaii in 1963 he was known as the "Dump Truck" because of his massive weight of 44.7st (284kg).

The oldest person graded to black belt

This goes to American Lucille "Killer" Thompson, who earned it in tae kwon do in 1984, aged 88! She was an active martial artist right up until her death in 1994.

Youngest black belt

Archie Gray, from Salisbury, UK, became Britain's youngest black belt in September 2007, at the age of six.

Cement-breaking records

Americans Drew Serrano and Colin Thompson jointly hold the record for breaking the most number of 2in (5mm) thick cement slabs with just one strike. At the US Open Martial Arts Championships 2004 they each broke 16 slabs. American Dan Netherland broke 55, 3in (7.3cm) thick concrete blocks, arranged in stacks of ten, in 17.5sec in 2003.

Enduro power

Not many people have heard of Paddy Doyle, but those in the know believe the former paratrooper to be one of the greatest endurance athletes of all time. As well as his martial arts records he holds 171 different records, including world records for the most one-handed push-ups in an hour (2,521),

The highest effective kick

Frenchman Christopher Pinna broke a 1in (2.5cm) thick wooden board that was suspended 10ft (3.03m) above his head, in 1988.

The most broken wooden boards

Tomas Teige of Germany holds the record for breaking the most ¾in (18mm) wooden boards with his hand. In 2006 at ETF Euro-Cup 2006 tae kwon do & Martial Arts Championships in Kaltenkirchen (Germany), Teige broke eight stacked boards, which were stacked directly on top of each other.

Hourly rate

The greatest number of full-contact, straight-arm punches struck in a single hour is 29,850. This equates to 497 every minute, or eight per second. This record is held by Briton Paddy Doyle. Paddy also holds the world record for full contact martial art kicks (5,750) and the fastest 110-man kumite (freestyle sparring or fighting), in which he defeated 110 black belt opponents in 3h 8min.

marathon running wearing a 50lb (22.5kg) backpack (5h 4min); and coal-bag carrying 110lb (49.5kg) 149 times up and down a 27yd (25m) course in one hour.

Most coconuts

German Muhamed Kahrimanovic beat the record for most coconuts smashed in one minute when he smashed 69, in 2005.

Phone jam

On 2 April 2007, 16 people crammed into a phone box in Pennan, Scotland, UK. The previous record of jamming people into a phone box had been 14, including 2 children. Of the 16 participants in the new world record, all were children.

Holding hands in protest

On 11 December 2004, the Bangladesh Awami League formed a human chain 652 miles (1,050km) long to oppose their government. Over five million people held hands from Teknaf to Tentulia, Bangladesh.

Longest human ice-skating chain

On 11 January 2008, in Mexico City, more than 225 children aged 8 to 15 formed the longest human ice-skating chain in the world.

Lots of learning

The largest school is the City Montessori School in Lucknow, India. For the 2007–2008 school year, 32,114 students enroled.

Racing gorillas

On 25 September 2005, a record 637 people dressed as gorillas gathered in London for the Great Gorilla Fun Run to raise money for The Dian Fossey Gorilla Fund. Fossey studied eight gorilla groups in Rwanda where she was killed on 2 December 1985 by an unknown attacker.

Luck of the Irish

On 4 August 2007, the world's largest Irish dance had 10,036 participants. The dance took place in Dublin ... Dublin, Ohio, USA, that is! Irish dancers led participants in a jig that lasted more than five minutes. The instructors taught from seven stages in the 27-acre festival.

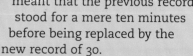

Tea or coffee? Tea please!

On 24 February 2007, 32,681 people drank powdered green tea in Indore, India. They even raised £6,231 ($12,462) for the city. One thousand volunteers served the tea and an electronic counting machine kept track of the number of participants.

Balloon jump

In Markelo in the Netherlands, 20 people parachuted from a balloon at the same time on 10 May 2003. They were 6,561ft (2,000m) in the air in a giant Cameron A-530 balloon, the largest passenger balloon in the world. Ten minutes later, ten more skydivers jumped from the same balloon. This meant that the previous record stood for a mere ten minutes before being replaced by the new record of 30.

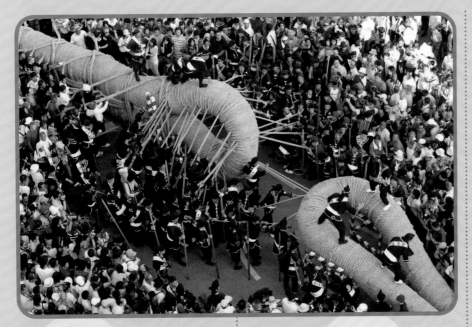

Tug of war

In Japan, the Naha tug-of-war is the largest tug-of-war event in the world, with 25,000 people attending in 1997! The tug-of-war symbolizes the struggles between countries in the East and the West.

People in a bubble

On 24 November 2007, 50 UK children, each over 5ft (1.5m), squeezed onto a stage encircled by a moat of soapy water. Then, bubbleologist Sam Heath enclosed them with an 11ft (3.4m) high tall, 5ft (1.5m) across wide bubble, setting a new world record!

Caziques!

In 2004, the National Scrabble Championship in the US had a record-breaking 837 entrants. Dr. Saladin Khoshnaw set the highest known score for a word in a Scrabble competition in 1982. He scored 392 points for the word "caziques," meaning Indian chief.

Vertical marathon

1,400 people scaled the 51-storey Temasek Towers, Singapore, China, on 21 November 2005.

Largest toy duck race

In 2002, a total of 123,000 toy ducks raced each other in The Great Singapore Duck Race, which took place in the Singapore River.

Dance dance dance

The longest conga line ever was at the Island School in Hong Kong. On 25 September 2007, 1,048 people got down to the song "YMCA".

Greatest number of strumming guitars

In 2007, 1,802 guitarists played Deep Purple's "Smoke on the Water" in Leinfelden-Echterdingen, Germany, breaking the previous record, 1,730.

Elton flamboyantly 50

Elton John had pop music's most flamboyant 50th birthday in 1997: an $80,000 (£40,000) Louis XIV dress, 500 guests. In the 1970s, Sir Elton wore a $10,000 (£5,000) pair of glasses with his name in flashing lights, and dressed as the Statue of Liberty, Donald Duck, and Mozart.

Most outrageous wedding dress

In 2005, Martin Katz, a jeweler who specializes in rare jewels, and Renee Strauss, a bridal couture designer, created the world's most extreme wedding dress. It cost $12 million (£5.5 million) and had 150 carats of diamonds. It is not known if anyone actually bought the dress.

3,000
diamonds on the most expensive dress

The most expensive designer dress

This record goes to the Scott Henshall creation worn by singer Samantha Mumba to the world premier of *Spider-Man II* in 2004, featuring 3,000 diamonds arranged in a spider's web shape. The gown was valued at a cool $10 million.

The most outrageous price tag

The world's most expensive suit was unveiled in London's Pall Mall in 2009. The "Alexander Amosu" (named after the designer himself) cost $100,000 (£65,000). Each suit is a one-off creation of platinum and gold threads, the rarest silks, and a blend of Himalayan Pashmina, qiviuk, and vicuna. To complete the garment are nine 18-carat gold and pave set diamond buttons.

Most expensive shoes

The most expensive pair of shoes were by Stuart Weitzman, who creates a new pair for the Oscars each year, for "Cinderellas". In 2006, Oscar-nominee Kathleen York wore his creation – "Rita Hayworth Heels": open-toe stilettos around a pair of earrings owned by legend Rita Hayworth, with rubies, sapphires, diamonds. The most expensive pair of non-bejeweled shoes was by Manolo Blahnik. His alligator boots, at $14,000 (£9,100), are just the thing if the Cinderella Slippers are out of your price range.

The tallest platform shoes

Elton John wore a 49ft (15m) tall pair for his role as Pinball Wizard in the 1975 movie *Tommy*.

Celebrity clothing

The high street and its shoppers have been slaves to big designer names ever since 2004 when high-end designer Karl Lagerfeld became the first such designer to produce a range of clothes specifically for the high street. He produced a range of clothing for H&M and, since then, designers like Stella McCartney, Viktor and Rolf, Roberto Cavalli, and artists, models, and actors such as Madonna, Kate Moss, and Kylie Minogue have all come up with their own individual labels.

Bring your own bottle!

Right next to the Pacific Ocean, the biggest body of water in the world, you'll find the Atacama Desert. Along

Monsoon winds

The term "monsoon" was first used to describe the seasonal winds blowing into the Indian subcontinent from the Arabian Sea and the Indian Ocean. The monsoon in the Indian subcontinent dwarfs the one in North America.

Bring an umbrella!

Mawsynram, India, is the wettest place on Earth, with average annual rainfall of 467in (11,873mm). To its east, Cherrapunji holds the monthly record: 366in (9,299mm) in July 1861.

Day of hurricanes

9 September is historically the day of greatest hurricane activity on the Gulf of Mexico.

the coast of Chile, South America, the Atacama is the driest place on Earth. This desert is over 20 million years old. While the nearby region of Antofagasta is said to have 0.03in (1mm) of rainfall per year, some weather stations in Atacama have never received rain. In fact, the area is so dry that it experienced no significant rainfall from 1570 to 1971!

World's deadliest hurricane

The deadliest recorded Atlantic hurricane is The Great Hurricane of 1780. Over 250,000 people perished, a death toll that exceeds the toll of any other entire decade of Atlantic hurricanes. The gusts hit Barbados at 199mph (320kph). The Great Hurricane was one of three exceptionally deadly storms occurring in October of 1780.

Hot Hot Hot!

On 13 September 1922, it reached 57.8°C (136°F) in El Azizia in Libya – the hottest temperature ever recorded on Earth.

El Niño

El Niño is one of the world's most famous weather phenomenons. It is caused by regular fluctuations of the ocean temperature in the tropical Pacific Ocean. It affects weather patterns around the globe. In 1982/83, a major El Niño impacted the globe so significantly that everyone learned about its importance. There were droughts throughout Africa, Australia, Central America, the Soviet Union, Southern Africa, and northeast Brazil. There were floods in Kenya and cyclones in the Pacific. The droughts of this time cost between $8–15 billion (£4–7.6 billion) damage worldwide.

Windiest

Commonwealth Bay in Antarctica is the windiest place on Earth. In 1912, Australian explorer Douglas Mawson recorded winds of 199mph (320kph). Mawson was a member of the first team to ever reach the South Magnetic Pole and led the party home!

Toyotorization

Dust storms in the Sahara have increased tenfold in 50 years, with 2-3 billion tons of dust being carried away each year. This is due to climate change as well as the replacement of the camel by four-wheel-drive vehicles.

Don't blow away!

On 12 April 1934, a gust of 231mph (372kph) was recorded on the summit of Mount Washington, the all-time surface wind speed record.

The Mistral

The Mistral, an atmospheric phenomenon in France, is a cold, strong wind, blowing in the winter and spring. The Mistral explains the unusually sunny climate of Provence. While other parts of France have clouds and storms, in Provence, the mistral clears the skies, allowing 2,700– 2,900 hours of sunshine per year.

Strongest lightning

On 27 January 2006 scientists tracked the strongest lightning storm ever. It was detected on the planet Saturn. At 2,174 miles (3,500km) wide, the storm was larger than the USA, with lightning that was 1,000 times stronger than lightning on Earth.

Lightning strikes

Lightning kills more people in Florida than in any other US state. It claims about 10 lives a year, about 10 per cent of the national total. Some open spaces in Florida have had lightning warning devices instaled, so that when lightning is detected within a 5m (8km) radius an alarm sounds and people can get undercover.

Don't ever come back

When Mark Spitz came back for the 1992 Olympics, aged 41, he didn't make one qualifying time, yet all his times were faster than his 1972 world records!

The first woman Channel swimmer

Gertrude Ederle (US) was the first female across the 19.2-mile (31-km) English Channel, in 1926. She swam from Dover to Calais, aged 19, in 14h 31min, beating the men's time by two hours. Her record stood for 35 years. The women's record from 2006 is Yvetta Hlavacova with 7h 25min 15sec.

Youngest Channel swimmer

When Lynne Cox was just 15 years old, in 1972, she became the youngest person to swim the English Channel. At that time she also completed the challenge in record time, but that record has since been broken.

Deep sea dive

When diving off the coast of California, in August 2006, US Navy diver Daniel Jackson set the deepest deep sea dive record of 2,000ft (610m).

Part-man part-fish?

Mark Spitz of the USA is considered to be the greatest swimmer of modern times. Between 1965 and 1972, Spitz set 33 world records, won nine Olympic golds, five Pan-American Games golds, and ten Maccabiah Games golds. At the time, his seven golds at the 1972 Olympics (100m freestyle, 100m butterfly, 200m butterfly, 200m freestyle, 4x100m freestyle relay, 4x100m medley relay, 4x200m freestyle relay) was a record at a single games. But the extraordinary Michael Phelps of the USA finally broke Spitz's long-standing record at the 2008 Olympics in Beijing. Phelps won gold in every single event he entered, setting a new record of 8 golds at a single Olympics and beaitng Spitz's previous mark.

Channel crossing

American George Brunstad was the oldest man to swim the English channel. He achieved this feat in 2004 when he was aged 70 years and four days.

The fastest crossing

Petar Stoychev, from Bulgaria, holds the record for the swimming across the English Channel. He made it across in 6h 57min 50 sec, in August 2007.

Coldest swim

Englishman Lewis Gordon Pugh holds the cold water swimming record; in July 2007 he became the first man to swim 0.6m (1km) at the North Pole. In a water temperature of -1.7°C (29°F), it took him 18min 50sec.

Open water scuba dive

The deepest such dive took place in the Mediterranean Sea, off the coast of Corsica in July 2005, when Pascal Bernabé descended to a depth of 1,083ft (330m). The longest open water dive happened when American Jerry Hall stayed under for 71h 39min 4`osec, in August 2002, in a lake in Tennessee, USA.

Cliff diving

In 1987, Swiss Oliver Favre pulled off a double back somersault from a record-breaking height of 187ft (53.90m) in Villiers-le-Lac, France. For women, the record is 121ft (36.80m), set by American Lucy Wardle in Hong Kong in 1985. In order to achieve higher take-offs and more spectacular dives, cliff diving is now done out of helicopters.

Endurance swimming

Endurance swimming began on 16 July 1998, when American Benoit Lecomte set off from Cape Cod in the US to swim 3,480 miles (5,600km) across the Atlantic. After swimming between six and eight hour stretches, alternated with two-hour naps in his support boat, Benoit walked ashore at Quiberon in France on 28 September, an incredible 72 days later.

Tightrope across Niagara

The first woman to walk across Niagara Falls on a tightrope was an Italian called Maria Spelterini who was born in 1853. She walked over the 170ft (52m) drop into the rapids below on a 2.5in (6.3cm) thick wire in a series of crossings in July 1876. For each crossing she added something new to the danger. She walked backwards, wore a blindfold, put peach baskets on her feet, and had her ankles and wrists manacled.

Swallowing swords record

Nine fearless people from the Sword Swallowers' Association International gathered together

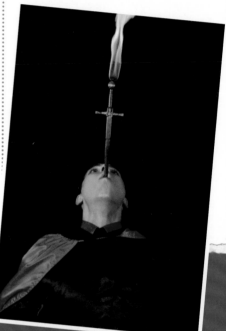

52
swords swallowed simultaneously

The first flight of the escapologist

Harry Houdini (1874–1926), the most famous escapologist in history, made the first controled, powered flight over Australia on 18 March 1910, at Digger's Rest in Victoria. He achieved this record flying a Voisin biplane purchased in Germany, for $5,000 (£2,500), and proudly claimed the world remember the aviator even if it forgot the escapalogist.

in Wilkes-Barre, Pennsylvania, USA, on 2 September 2005 to simultaneously swallow an amazing 52 swords, beating the previous world record of 50. Australia's leading sword swallower Matthew Henshaw holds the individual world record for swallowing the most swords at once, at 14.

Very hot feat

Scott Bell from the UK walked on burning hot embers in his bare feet for a total distance of 328ft (100m) in the city of Wuxi in Southern China, on 28 November 2006. Remarkably, his feet were not burned and he was completely unharmed during this record-breaking feat.

Riding on a lion's back

The Russian brothers Edgar and Askold Zapashny hold the record for the longest jump riding on the back of a lion. They jumped 7ft 6in (2.3m) on the back of a lion called Michael while performing for the Russian State Circus Company in Perm on 28 July 2006.

Escaping from handcuffs under water

Czech magician and escapologist Zdenek Bradac holds the world record for the fastest escape from handcuffs while submerged under water. He set the record at the Jablonec swimming pool in Jablonec nad Nisou, Czech Republic, on 9 September 2009, when he managed to escape in an incredible 10.66 seconds.

The real Spiderman

Frenchman Robert Alain has climbed up so many tall buildings, including skyscrapers, that he has earned his nickname of

Frozen in time

Israeli entertainer Hezi Dayan emerged from a record-breaking 64 hours in an 8-ton (8,000kg) block of ice, in Tel Aviv's central Rabin Square, on 1 January 2010. He beat David Blaine's record set in 2000, when Blaine had frozen himself within a 6-ton (5,500kg) block for 63 hours 42 minutes, afterwards unable to walk for a month. They both survived the threat of blood clots, frostbite, and hypothermia.

Highest balloon skywalk

On 1 September 2004, Mike Howard walked along a beam, just a couple of inches thick, which was suspended between two hot air balloons. He was 21,400ft (6,522m) up in the sky over Yeovil, UK, and he didn't even have a parachute to help save him if he fell off. He kept his nerve, though, and broke his own world record for the highest altitude balloon skywalk.

"Spiderman". Alain has scaled the exterior of more than 80 buildings without the help of any ropes, pulleys, harnesses or safety nets. However, he has suffered a number of serious falls and now says that he suffers from a fear of heights!

The Pharaoh's tomb

The most famous discovery in the history of archeology was the finding of the tomb of the Egyptian pharaoh Tutankhamen. British archeologists Lord Carnarvon (1866–1923) and Howard Carter

(1874–1939) found the tomb in the Valley of the Kings in Luxor in 1922. Unlike most Egyptian tombs, it hadn't been emptied by tomb-robbers. It was full of dazzling gold including a burial mask and precious artworks. Tutankhamen ruled Egypt for just nine years and was only 18 when he died in about 1323BCE.

The greatest multi-city find

When German archeologist Heinrich Schliemann (1822–90) became the first person to unearth the city of Troy in Northwest Turkey between 1874 and 1890, he found not just one ancient city, but nine. Each of the cities had been built on top of the previous one. The oldest of the cities dates from about 3,000BCE, while the most recent is from the 1st century BCE. The seventh city is believed to date from the time of the Trojan War of about 1250BCE, which was described in Homer's *Iliad*.

Teenage discovery

Four teenagers discovered the Lascaux cave system, near Montignac in France, in 1940. It is one of the most important finds of pre-historic human life and features some of the oldest cave paintings ever found, dating from about 15,000BCE. There are 2,000 pictures including horses, deer, buffalo, and a human. The cave was open to the public but the condition of the paintings began to deteriorate so they were closed again in 1963. Visitors can visit a copy of the real cave, called Lascaux II, which was built in 1983 into a hillside close to the original caves.

Most preserved city

The ancient Roman city of Pompeii became frozen in time in AD79 when the volcano Vesuvius erupted. It killed most of the residents and buried the city under ash, preserving it. When the city was accidentally rediscovered in 1748, the city was just like it was at the moment of the disaster.

Terracotta warriors

The largest exhibition of The Terracotta Army outside of China took place at the British Museum between September 2007 and April 2008. The discovery of the burial chamber was one of the most significant finds of the twentieth century. Found in Xi'an by local farmers in 1974, 7,000 life-size warriors made from terracotta clay were buried alongside China's first emperor, Qin in 210BCE.

The home of the Minotaur

British amateur archeologist, Arthur Evans (1851–1941), excavated Knossos, the chief city of Minoan Crete, over a 36-year period from 1899. It is the largest Bronze Age site on the island of Crete. Evans first uncovered the palace of King Minos, dating from around 2,000BCE, and a maze of rooms, which is allegedly the labyrinth of the Minotaur, a half-man and half-bull monster that killed boys and girls.

Understanding the ancients

The Rosetta Stone, found by Napoleon Bonaparte's soldiers in Egypt in 1799, is a slab of stone dating from 196BCE which has the same message written in three

languages: Greek, demotic, and hieroglyphics. After the discovery of the slab the Greek writing helped researchers understand Egyptian hieroglyphics for the first time.

The speedy dragonfly

The Austrophlebia costalis, an Australian dragonfly, is the fastest insect, reaching speeds of 36mph (57.9kph) over short distances. It was once recorded flying downhill at 61mph (98kph). Dragonflies have two sets of wings to help them fly fast and they move with great agility.

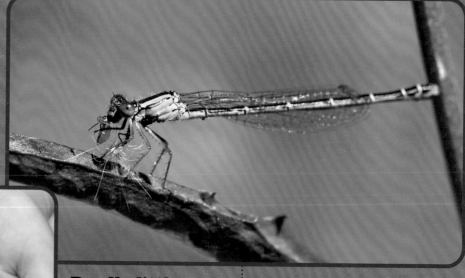

Deadly little stingers

The insects that have the most potent venom are harvester ants from the Pogonomyrmex genus. The venom is more potent than that of a bee and only a few snakes have more lethal venom. However, the ant releases such a small amount that it would take hundreds of stings to kill a human. The sting of the honeybee kills more people than that of any other insect, but the deaths are due to an allergic reaction rather than the strength of the venom.

Flea infestation

The largest known flea is the Hystrichopsylla schefferi – a flea found in the nest of a mountain beaver in Washington State, USA. In the UK, the largest ever-recorded infestation of human fleas was found at a pig farm in 1986. It reportedly turned an area the size of a tennis court brown and it is estimated that in order to cover an area of that size, this particular species of flea must have numbered about 133,378,450.

30
minutes – lifespan of mayfly

The many-legged millipede

Millipede means "a thousand feet" but no insects really have got that many legs. The Illacme plenipes millipede holds the record, though, with one specimen having 750 legs. This millipede was thought to have become extinct in the 1920s, but was recently rediscovered in California, USA.

Tough exteriors

All insects have a hard shell over their bodies, but beetles have the hardest shells, giving them amazing protection from predators and stopping them from being crushed. There are 350,000 different species and the goliath beetle, named after the biblical giant, is the biggest of them all. It is the heaviest flying insect, weighing over 3.5oz (100g).

Long live the queen!

The African termite Macrotermes bellicosus reaches a length of 5in (13cm) at maturity, and is the world's largest termite. The queen can live for up to 50 years and the whole termite colony is built around her, because she is the sole reproductive machine, laying up to 2,000 eggs every day.

Shortest lifespan

Some species of adult mayflies only live for half-an-hour. However, they can live as naiads – which is what they are called before they are fully-grown – for about a year. The naiads live in streams until they grow wings and become fully adult. As adults, their sole purpose before they die is to mate, so they do not even eat anything.

No real appetite

The Attacus Atlas, otherwise known as the Atlas moth, is the largest moth in the world. It has a wing span of 1ft (0.3m) and can easily be mistaken for a small bird when it's flying around. The moth comes from the jungles of Southeast Asia and is born without a mouth. It has just two weeks to find a mate before literally starving to death.

The longest insect

The Phobaeticus chani, a stick insect from Sabah in Borneo, is the longest insect. It has a full length of 22.32in (56.7cm). Its eggs are also unique, with wing-like extensions on either side to help them drift, aiding the species to spread.

Earliest evidence of electricity

There is evidence to suggest that electricity was understood in the Middle East as early as 1200BCE, with the discovery of the so-called Baghdad Battery, an ancient object that resembles a modern battery in its metallic construction.

The first electric arc

Humphry Davy, an English scientist, made the first electric light in 1800. He experimented with electricity and invented an electric battery. When he connected wires to his battery and a piece of carbon, the carbon glowed, producing light. This is called an electric arc.

Don't try this at home

Benjamin Franklin was the first man to demonstrate how electricity could be harnessed, in 1752. He

attached his house key to the dampened string of a kite and flew it in a thunderstorm, observing how the current in the air charged the kite as sparks jumped from the key to the back of his hand.

Water power

On 30 September 1882, the world's first hydroelectric power plant began operation on the Fox River in Appleton, Wisconsin. The plant, which was later named the Appleton Edison Light Company, was inspired by Thomas Edison's plans for an electricity-producing station in New York, and was instigated by Appleton paper manufacturer, H.F. Rogers.

1752
electricity first harnessed by Benjamin Franklin

The electric car

Robert Anderson of Scotland invented the first crude electric carriage, thought to have been sometime between 1832 and 1839. A small-scale electric car was designed by Professor Stratingh of Groningen, Holland, and built by his assistant Christopher Becker in 1835.

... Eureka!!

The battery was invented by Italian physicist Count Alessandro Voltaire in 1800, when he discovered that two electrodes, one made of zinc the other of copper, in a solution of sulphuric acid, salt, and water, could hold an electric current and deliver it in a steady flow.

The first electric trams

Electric-powered trams would traditionally gather power from an unshielded overhead wire. In 1880 the first electric streetcar was invented and tested by Fyodor Pirotsky, in St Petersburg, Russia. The first successful electric tramline to run in America was the Richmond Union Passenger Railway, which was built by. Frank J. Sprague, in Richmond, Virginia.

The world's biggest battery

This is found in Fairbanks, Alaska, where the earthquake-proof rechargeable battery occupies 21,527 sq ft (2,000 sq m) – that's bigger than a football pitch – and weighs 2,866,000lb (1,300 tonnes). It is capable of supplying power to the whole city of 12,000 people for around seven minutes, which is enough time to start the emergency generators in the event of a power failure.

A bright spark

Thomas Edison is credited with inventing the light bulb because it was his efforts with developing a durable, bright-burning carbon fiber filament that produced an efficient, commercially affordable bulb that could be easily mass produced. More importantly, however, Edison invented the first widely accessible electric power distribution system. In 1882, he switched on the power at the Edison Electric Illuminating Company, at his Pearl Street Power Station, and supplied 110 volts of current to 59 buildings in New York City. Edison also set up the first electricity generating station in Britain, with the steam-powered Holborn Viaduct station in London, which supplied power for streetlights in the immediate area.

What is snooker?

A very popular game in the UK, snooker is played with 15 red balls, worth one point each, and six balls of different colors and different values. The object of the game is for each player to try to pot as many red balls as possible, going for a colored ball each time he does.

Hendry the hero

Scotland's Stephen Hendry became the youngest snooker World Champion on 29 April 1990, when he won the title aged 21 years 106 days. He is the player who has won the most first-class titles, a total of 36, and the longest unbeaten run in competition from 17 March 1990 to 13 January 1991, winning five major titles and 36 individual matches. Stephen also holds the record for largest number of 100 plus scores in a single tournament, when he notched up five on his way to the final of the 2002 World Championship. Ronnie O'Sullivan

holds the highest number of 147 breaks made in competition – nine (breaking Hendry and O'Sullivan's jointly held record of eight.)

The longest day

The 1985 World Snooker Championship final between Steve Davis and Dennis Taylor lasted 14h 50min. No other snooker game, or final, has lasted as long.

The longest snooker frame

Shaun Murphy and Dave Harold contested the longest frame (each game consists of a set number of odd frames, or games) of snooker in a major competition.

During their match at the 2008 China Open, one frame lasted 93min and 12sec.

The fastest 147 break

This record goes to Ronnie "The Rocket" O'Sullivan with a time of 5min 20sec, which he achieved in 1997. Ronnie also holds the other four fastest 147 times in the game.

Making a break

Steve Davis made the first televized maximum break of 147 in 1982, while the youngest player to make a maximum 147 in competition was 19-year-old Ding Junhui at the 2007 Masters tournament.

Highest competiton break

This honor goes to the UK's Chris Carbutt in 1998, when, thanks to fouls by his opponent Tony Drago, he made a break of 149.

Did you know?

In the US, pool or "pocket billiards" is the second most popular participant sport, after 10-pin bowling. "Pool" is the term used for a family of games played on a specific class of billiards table, having six pockets. "Pocket billiards" is almost exclusively referred to as pool, due to its unfortunate association with "poolrooms" where gamblers "pooled" their money, betting remotely on horse races.

What is pool?

Pool is a cue sport played with a set number of balls on a table with six pockets. 8-ball and 9-ball pool are

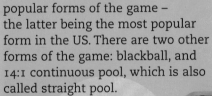

popular forms of the game – the latter being the most popular form in the US. There are two other forms of the game: blackball, and 14:1 continuous pool, which is also called straight pool.

The longest run in straight pool

This record is held by Willie Mosconi of Philadelphia, Pennsylvania (1913-1993) who sunk 526 consecutive balls, without a miss, in an exhibition match of 14:1 continuous pool in Springfield, Ohio, in 1954. Many in the game believe this record is unbeatable.

Billiards' most famous followers

The history of billiards is rich: the body of Mary, Queen of Scots, was wrapped in her billiard table cover; the dome of Thomas Jefferson's home in Monticelli conceals a billiard room, as the game was then illegal in Virginia; it is mentioned in Shakespeare's *Antony and Cleopatra*; while enthusiasts have included Mozart, Louis XIV, and Lewis Carroll who longed for a circular table.

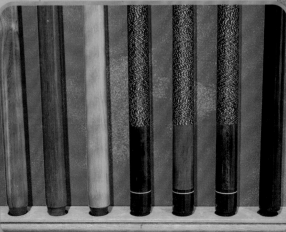

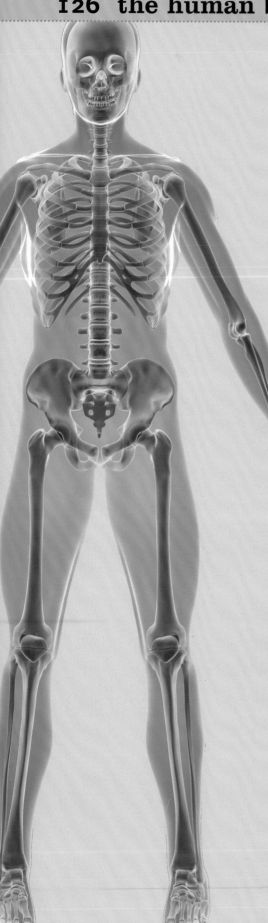

Long bones

The femur bone is the longest bone in the human body. It is also called the thighbone. The word femur is the Latin term for thigh, which has been derived from another Latin word, femoris. Apart from being the largest bone in the body, it is also the strongest bone of the human body. The femur is the part of the leg above the knee and stops at the hip.

Small bones

The smallest bones in the human body are the ear ossicles, three bones that are found in the middle ear. They are called the stapes (also called the "stirrup"), incus (or the "anvil"), and malleus (sometime referred to as the "hammer").

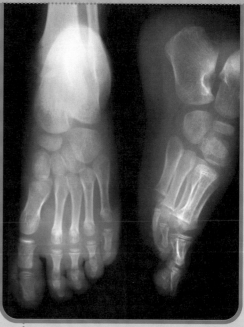

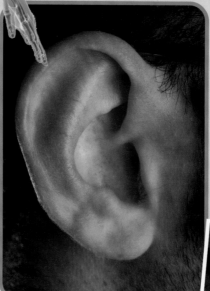

The toe bone's connected to the....

Bones are a specialized, rigid connective tissue. The point where bones connect is called a joint. Ankle sprains are the most common joint injury worldwide. In 2006, there were 20 million ankle sprains in the US, making up 20 per cent of all US sports injuries.

Skier's knee

For a skier, the most vulnerable part of the body is the knee, which accounts for some 45 per cent of all skiing injuries. The most common knee injury seen in skiing is the anterior cruciate ligament injury.

Old bones

The oldest known hominid skeleton was found in Ethiopia, in Africa, and has been dated at 4.4 million years.

Boarder's wrist

Snowboarders around the world suffer an estimated 95,000 wrist fractures every season. In fact, 22 per cent of all snowboarding accidents are wrist injuries. It is the most common upper body injury because beginners, in particular, try to learn a stable stance on their snowboard. Unlike skiers, who can step out a leg when they lose balance, snowboarders are more likely to topple over and to fall onto an out-stretched hand.

Most common skateboarding injury

Almost all medical reports agree that greater than 60 per cent of skateboarding injuries occur in the hands and arms, and the wrist. Much like those which result from

accidents while snowboarding and inline skating, these wrist injuries occur while the skateboarder is attempting to cushion a fall. According to the National Safety Council (in the US) over 50,000 skateboarding injuries are treated in emergency rooms each year, and this record number is number increasing every year due to the increasing popularity of the sport.

Breaking, growing, mending

The first X-ray photograph was of inventor Wilhelm Röntgen's wife's hand. The image displayed both her wedding ring and her bones. Röntgen discovered radiation "X-Rays" on 8 November 1895, which enabled us to see bone structure – altering the course of medicine forever. On 18 January 1896, H.L. Smith formally displayed his X-ray machine. Though bones are very tough, they can sometimes break, but do heal. Once healed, they are stronger than ever before.

Joint replacement

By far the most common form of joint replacement is that of the hip. The earliest recorded attempts at hip replacement were carried out in Germany, and used ivory to replace the femoral head (the ball on the femur).

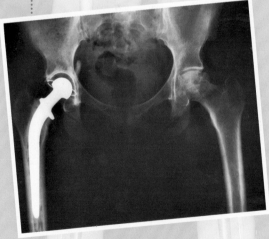

4.4 million years - oldest skeleton

Largest SFX model used in a movie

Superman: The Movie featured the biggest model ever built for a film, a 7ft (2.1m) long recreation of San Francisco's Golden Gate Bridge.

First fully computer generated film

This record goes to *Toy Story*, made by Pixar for Disney in 1995. Its success revived the animated movie business to put films like *Shrek* and *Finding Nemo* into the all-time box office Top 20.

First digital 3-D movie

This record is held by *Chicken Little*, made in 2005. The movie was also unique because it didn't have to be viewed through polarizing spectacles or in a special cinema.

The first realistic example of CGI animation in a movie

In *Young Sherlock Holmes*, in 1985, the character of the Stained Glass Knight had to appear to come to life out of a church window. Up until then, in films like *Tron* and *The Last Starfighter*, CGI characters always looked like they were produced on a computer.

The most expensive special effects film

This record goes to *Pirates of the Caribbean: At World's End*, which cost its makers a staggering $300,000,000 (£195,000,000). It took two SFX firms five months of intense work to create the ground-breaking water-based effects.

20,000
extras employed to act in Lord of the Rings

The first use of natural human movement for a CGI character

This was in 1991, in *Terminator 2: Judgement Day*, when pioneering motion capture techniques meant the robots could be seen to move just like their flesh and blood counterparts.

Most expensive SFX movie ever made

This is *Avatar*. In the 2010 movie, directed by James Cameron and staring Sam Worthington, the creation of a CGI world cost in excess of a whopping $200 million (£130 million).

Before computers took over

Before SFX technology, the most reliable way to achieve realistic special effects was with models and "stop-motion". This means the filming is stopped while the models are moved, then starts again to give the impression of motion. The first master of this technique was Ray Harryhausen, who created the monsters and the effects for such early action classics as *Clash of the Titans*, *The Seventh Voyage of Sinbad*, *Jason and the Argonauts*, and *One Million Years BC*. He won a Lifetime Achievement Oscar in 1992.

SFX in Middle Earth

The Lord of the Rings trilogy has an effect in almost every scene. There was a year spent in post-production on SFX alone, and it is believed they cost over $100 million (£65

The biggest water tank

It's no surprise that this record is held by the movie *Titanic*, which was released in 1997. The production team on the movie created an enormous eight-acre, 17-million gallon tank in the Pacific Ocean at Rosarito Beach in Mexico. Then, as the water had to be clear in order for the under-water filming to take place, it was necessary for the team to install a custom-built filtration system capable of cleaning 6,000 gallons (27 cubic meters) per minute. The movie won that year's Oscar for Best Visual Effects.

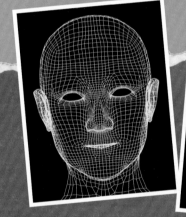

First sophisticated morphing techniques

The 1988 fantasy adventure film *Willow* convincingly faded one character or object out of another, although they had been employed crudely on the Eddie Murphy film *The Golden Child* two years earlier. In *Terminator 2: Judgement Day*, in 1991, characters seamlessly changed their appearance and the movie won that year's Oscar for Best Visual Effects.

million) for each film. As well as a computer-generated Gollum, the actors had to be digitally resized to create the correct heights for each character. The highlights were the battle sequences. In the scenes, 20,000 extras were employed, but a specially written computer program was still need to make the 20,000 seem like 200,000. The special program also allowed them to move and fight in smaller, independently-controlled, groups.

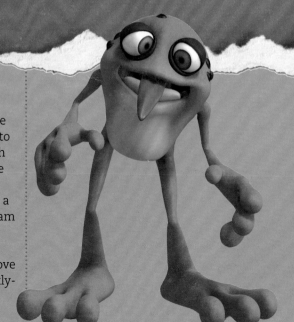

Star of Africa or Darya-I-Nur?

The Golden Jubilee Diamond is the largest cut diamond in the world. A yellow-brown diamond in a fire-rose cushion, it weighs 545.67 carats. Found in South Africa in 1985, the raw diamond weighed 755.5 carats. Now part of the Thai crown jewels, it was named by King Bhumibol Adulyadej of Thailand to mark the 50th anniversary of his coronation. The Darya-I-Nur diamond, weighing only 182 carats, is considered rarer still due to its unique color – an unusual pale pink.

Worth the curse?

The Hope Diamond is the largest gemstone of its kind ever found and resides in the Smithsonian Institute in Washington, D.C., USA. The Hope is a 45.52-carat blue diamond, estimated to be worth $350 million (£230 million). However, it is also thought to carry a curse that it will bring death to its possessor.

Amazing formations

In the Sahara Desert in Algeria, the biggest sand dunes are up to 1,410ft (430m) high – three times the largest Egyptian Pyramid, and 203ft (62m) shorter than the Shanghai World Financial Center, China. The Badain Jaran Dunes in China's Gobi Desert are the world's tallest stationary dunes, at 1,640ft (500m). China's Stone Forest – a strange and magnificent stone landscape – covers 15.4 sq miles (400 sq km), which includes an underground stone forest of 1.16 sq miles (3 sq km). Mexico's Cueva de los Cristales (Cave of Crystals) houses giant gypsum crystals. Some are over 37ft (11m) long! They are the largest crystals on Earth.

The diamond city

The earliest written record of diamond cutting comes from Antwerp in 1550, and the city has been at the centre of the world diamond industry since the 1600s. A record 80 per cent of the world's uncut diamonds are traded through the Belgian diamond exchange on Simonszstraat, and over 25 million carats of diamonds pass through the city every year.

Big gold

The largest single lump of gold ever discovered was found in Australia. It was the Holterman Nugget, and it was found in Hill End in NSW on 19 October 1872. The whole nugget weighed 518.3lb (235.1kg), with 205.7lb (93.3 g) of pure gold.

Most common

Copper is the most versatile and durable of all minerals, and it is everywhere. It's used in the production of computers, household appliances, water pipes, and electrical wiring. In New York City, USA, the Statue of Liberty contains 178,574lb (81,000kg) of copper!

metallic iron it must be smelted or sent through a reduction process to remove the oxygen. When this happens iron is left, which is the most commonly used metal in the world. China is the world largest producer of iron ore, uncovering 520 million metric tons (520 billion kgs) in 2006.

Most expensive diamond

A rare and flawless blue diamond is the most expensive precious jewel of its kind ever sold. The gem, which is 6.04 carats and sparkles with an unusual blue hue, was sold for $6.50 million (£4.25 million) at a Sotheby's auction in Hong Kong.

The biggest emerald

At 858 carats, the Gachala Emerald is the largest in the world. The crystal was found in 1967 at the Vega de San Juan mine in Columbia and is named after the mining district in which it was found. Famous NY Jeweler, Harry Winston, donated it to the Smithsonian Museum.

Fool's gold

The Federal Reserve Bank of New York is reputedly the largest gold repository in the world and holds about 5,000 metric tons (5,000,000kg) of gold bullion ($248 billion/£162 billion). The gold is owned by foreign nations, central banks, and international organizations. The Federal Reserve Bank does not own the gold but "protects" it at no charge.

Iron man

William A. Burt discovered iron ore on the Marquette Range in Michigan, USA, on 19 September 1844. To convert it to

The mother of all pearls

The largest and most expensive pearl ever to be found is known as the "Pearl of Lao Tzu," or the "The Pearl of Allah." It measures 9.45in (24cm) in diameter and weighs 14.1lb (1kg). It is approximately 31,893.5 carats and is valued at nearly $60 million (£39 million). The pearl was extracted from a giant clam off the coast of Palawan in 1934 by a Filipino diver.

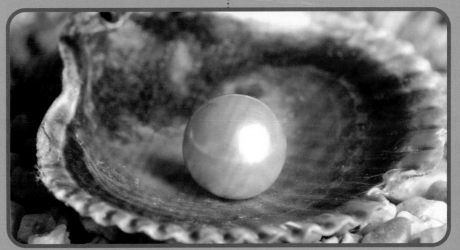

Discus records

Discus throwing is almost symbolic of the Olympic Games. One of the earliest competitive sports from Greece, evidence of it dates back to the 5th century BCE. The men's record for the discus is 243ft (74.08m), set by Germany's Jurgen Schult in 1986. The women's record, 252ft (76.8m) was set in 1989 by German Gabriele Reinsch.

World's best shot-putters

The men's world record for shot put is 75.85ft (23.12m), set by American Randy Barnes in 1990. For the women, the record is 74.25ft (22.63m), achieved by Natalya Lisovskaya in 1987.

Out of this world

At the 1968 Olympics in Mexico, American long jumper Bob Beamon set a record so far beyond the previous best he fell to his knees in shock when it was announced. He

Men's high jump world record

This is held by Cuban Javier Sotomayor, at 8.03ft (2.45m). The Cuban, who set the record in 1993 in Salamanca and is considered to be the best high jumper of all time, missed the 1984 and 1988 Olympic Games due to the Cuban boycott. The women's world record is 6.86ft (2.09m), set by Bulgarian Stefka Kostadinova in 1987 in Rome.

Flopping to fame

The technique that practically every high jumper uses these days – to jump backwards and flip over the bar – has only been in use for 40 years. The technique was first seen at the Mexico City Olympics in 1968 when the American Dick Fosbury won the gold medal and set a new world record of 7.34ft (2.24m), demonstrating a perfect use of the "Fosbury Flop."

had surpassed the record by 21.6 in (55cm) – all previous progressions had been less than 3.9in (10cm). His leap of 29.19ft (8.90m) was called the perfect jump. The record lasted 23 years, and has since been beaten only once. The current record of 29.36ft (8.95m) was set by American Mike Powell in 1991.

Longest female leap

The women's long jump record is 24.67ft (7.52m), as set by the Russian Galina Christyakova in Leningrad in July 1988.

New to the games

The javelin competition was only included in the Olympic Games in 1908 at the fourth Olympiad in London, and there was only a men's competition then. The women's competition was introduced in 1932. The current men's Olympic record was set by Jan Zelezny in Sydney in 2000 with a throw of 296ft (90.17m). In addition to the Olympic record, Jan Zelezny holds the current world record with a throw of 323ft (98.48m). Since 1936, the women's Olympic record has been broken 17 times. It is currently held by Osleidys Menéndez of Cuba. In Athens, Greece, in 2004, she threw her javelin a record-breaking 234.67ft (71.53m).

Why triple jump?

When triple jump first became an Olympic event – in the first modern Games in 1896 – it was known as "hop, hop, jump" as that was how the actions were performed. The current records for triple jump are, for men, 60ft (18.29m), set by Briton Jonathan Edwards in 1995; and, for women, 50.85ft (15.5m) by Ukrainian Inessa Kravets, set in 1995.

How pole vaulting started

Pole vaulting began as a way of crossing canals or marshy ground in the Fens of Lincolnshire, Cambridgeshire, and Huntingdonshire, in the UK – every household had a supply of jumping poles. Also, Venetian gondoliers used to tie their gondolas up away from the quayside, so they wouldn't get stolen, then vault ashore with their punting poles.

The pole vault world records

Sergei Bubka is the only athlete to win six consecutive World Championship titles and an Olympic gold. The current world records for this sport are 20.14ft (6.14m) for men and 16.43ft (5.01m) for women, set by, respectively, Ukrainian Bubka in 1994, and Russian Yelena Isinbayeva in 2005.

The world's strongest man

Mariusz Pudzianowski, a former gym insructor from Poland, has won the World's Strongest Man title the most number of times, securing it for the fifth time in 2008. Winning the competition involves a range of feats including pulling vehicles, carrying heavy barrels, and lifting huge stones. Mariusz Pudzianowski came second in 2009.

A man with a car on his head

In 24 May 1999, Britain's John Evans balanced a car on his head, without using his arms, for 33 seconds. He supported the whole weight of a Mini, which weighs about 352lb

King of push-ups

Roy Berger from Canada holds the world record for the most number of push-ups completed in one hour when he did 3,416 in Ottawa on 30 August 1998.

Record crazy

On 5 October 2006, Ashrita Furman set the fastest time for an individual to push a car for one mile (1.6km) when he completed the task of pushing a 4,150lb (1,882kg) van in 21min 8sec in Long Island, USA. The American also claims to be the person who holds the most records in the world. His wide-ranging feats include a variety of hopscotch, pogo-stick, and milk-crate balancing records.

3,416
push-ups in one hour

Pulling a car with your eyelids

Dong Changsheng from China broke the world record for the heaviest eyelid pull on 26 September 2006 in Changchun, Jilin Province. Better known as a kung-fu expert, Dong attached a rope to his bottom eyelids by means of hooks and pulled a car weighing 3,300lb (1,497kg) for 32ft (10m).

(160kg), by using his exceptionally strong neck muscles. The stunt was very dangerous because the car would have crushed him if it fell off, but luckily John Evans is a professional "head balancer." His other achievements include balancing 235 pints of beer, 429 cans of soda, 6 oil drums, and 101 bricks on his head.

World's strongest ear

Zafar Gill from Pakistan has the world's strongest ear. He lifted 136lb (61.7kg) of weights, using only his right ear, in Vienna, Austria, on 30 September 2007.

The strongest weightlifters

Hossein Rezazadeh of Iran holds the official world weightlifting record for the heaviest single lift. The "Iranian Hercules" can lift 469.6lb (213kg) using the "snatch" technique (lifting from platform to locked arms in one movement) and an amazing 579.8lb (263kg) using the "clean-and-jerk" method (where the weight rests on the shoulders midway through the lift). For the women, Shuangshuang Mu can snatch 306.4lb (139kg) and Gonghong Tang can clean-and-jerk 401.2lb (182kg).

A heavy chest

As if lying on a bed of nails wasn't challenging enough, American Chad Netherland did so with 26 blocks of concrete on his chest,

Man pulls airplane

Rev. Kevin Fast, a Lutheran Pastor from Ontario, Canada, pulled an aircraft weighing 416,299lb (188,830kg) over 28.9ft (8.8m) in 2009, setting a new world record. Fast broke David Huxley's record of 412,264lb (187,000kg), and set this record in a time of 1min 16sec. Fast also holds the record for heaviest vehicle pulled over 30.5m (100ft).

One-finger push-ups

Paul Lynch of Britain managed 124 consecutive one-finger push-ups on 21 April 1992.

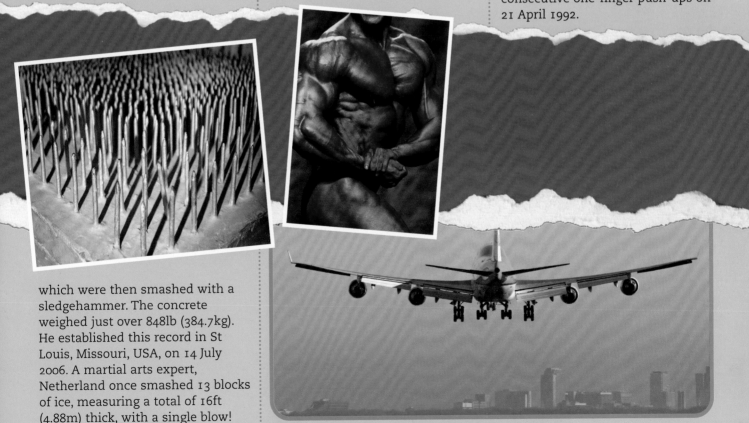

which were then smashed with a sledgehammer. The concrete weighed just over 848lb (384.7kg). He established this record in St Louis, Missouri, USA, on 14 July 2006. A martial arts expert, Netherland once smashed 13 blocks of ice, measuring a total of 16ft (4.88m) thick, with a single blow!

A man-made wonder

The Taj Mahal in India, completed in 1648, is architecture's best-known memorial to a wife. It was built by the ruler Shah Jahan, in loving memory of his wife Mumtaz Mahal. It is perfectly symmetrical and is covered with white marble. The Taj Mahal took 20,000 laborers 22 years to build. With a huge central dome and minarets on each corner, the mausoleum is by far the largest Islamic tomb ever destined for a woman.

Darth Vader's helmet

London's City Hall (above) has been called Darth Vader's helmet, a squashed egg, and a rugby ball. Like a sphere that has been pushed from one side, it is London's most energy-efficient building. It's 148ft (45m) high and has 25 per cent less surface area than a cubed building of the same volume. The design means that it's the most energy-efficient shape possible, which allows it to run on a quarter of the energy used normally by a conventional building of a similar size. It is designed by Foster & Partners who also built the famous "Gherkin," located nearby.

22 years to build the Taj Mahal

A house shaped like a boot

The weirdest house ever built is Haines Shoe House in Hellam, Pennsylvania, USA, which is shaped like a boot. Colonel Mahlon M. Haines owned 40 shoe stores and, in 1948, asked an architect to build a house shaped like a work boot to advertise his brand. Haines let the elderly and honeymooners stay in the boot house, who all went back with free pairs of shoes. It is now a museum, the first of its kind.

The dancing building

The dancers Fred Astaire and Ginger Rogers inspired Frank Gehry's The Dancing House (right), which was completed in Prague in 1996. Some people call it the Drunk House because it looks like it is slumped onto the adjoining buildings.

Flatiron Building in New York

New York's Flatiron Building is not the first building of its shape, it is the third, but it is the biggest of this particular style of building. When Daniel Burnham built the Flatiron Building in 1902, it was one of the first New York buildings to have a steel frame, and was one of the tallest structures (285ft/87m), but it became more famous because of its iron shape. Ingeniously, it makes the most of the triangular lot it was built on. It was meant to be called the Fuller Building, but locals renamed it the Flatiron.

The building that stays white

The Sacré-Coeur Basilica in Paris, completed in 1914, is unlike any other large church in France. All-white and featuring three domes, including a massive 272ft (83m) central one, the church looms over the Montmartre area of Paris like a huge wedding cake. Its brilliant white exterior never fades, despite city pollution, because it is constructed of travertine stone, which reacts with rainwater to create calcite, which acts like bleach. It is the largest building using this material in Paris. Other notable buildings using travertine extensively include the Colosseum in Rome, and the Getty Center in Los Angeles, California.

The building that changed a city

Architect Frank Gehry's Guggenheim Museum in Bilbao, an industrial city in northern Spain, is one of the country's most unusual buildings. The museum is formed of a curving titanium-metal-covered structure unlike anything anyone had seen before. Eighty per cent of tourists go to Bilbao simply to see the museum. The building, which opened in 1997, became so famous that people started traveling to Bilbao just to see it. It changed the fortunes of the city so much that architects and economists now talk about the "Bilbao effect." This now-established model, which started in Bilbao, has been copied in other cities in order to build up their economies.

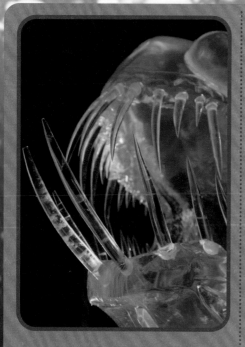

The deepest of the deep

The deepest place in the ocean is the Mariana Trench. Situated in the Pacific Ocean, it is over 6.8 miles (11km) deep. Despite the pressure of all that water on top of them, fish such as the flounder, sole, and shrimp still live there, breaking the record for the deepest-dwelling fish in the world.

As vicious as a viper

The viperfish is one of the fiercest fish in the deep and also one of the least attractive. Like a viper snake, it has a thin body, a big head, and vicious long fangs. It waits at the bottom of the ocean until it is dark and then it rises nearer the surface to hunt its prey. It feasts on small fish and crustaceans, which don't stand a chance once they get trapped between the viperfish's sharp teeth. Viperfish are mostly about 12in (30cm) long, but specimens up to 80in (2m) long have been found.

The frightening fangtooth

If any deep-sea fish can rival the vipertooth for unattractiveness, it is the fangtooth. It is less than 6in (15cm) long but, proportionate to its body size, it has the largest teeth of any fish in the oceans. Its

teeth are so long that it has had to evolve two holes on either side of its brain to accommodate the fangs when it shuts its mouth.

The poisonous octopus

The most venomous mollusc is the blue-ringed octopus. It may only be 1.2in (3cm) long and its bite doesn't really hurt, but the octopus kills more people than sharks. Each one holds enough venom to kill ten people and there is no antidote. It lives in tide pools in the Pacific Ocean, so watch where you are putting your toes!

The super squid

The largest squid is called the colossal squid and it is the world's largest invertebrate. It is estimated to be 39.46ft (12.14m) long and also

has the largest eyes in the world. The colossal squid is believed to hunt by bioluminescence, which means that it can create its own light source in order to attract and see its prey. It has hooks on the end of its tentacles in order to fight off whales.

Amazing male pregnancy

Male seahorses compete with each other to become pregnant! The male puts the female's eggs in its pouch and gives birth to up to 2,000 babies a few weeks later.

The little stinger

The smallest jellyfish is also the deadliest. The irukandji is less than 1in (2.7cm) tall but its sting causes irukandji syndrome – where you suffer excruciating pain to the kidneys and muscles, vomiting, and a burning sensation on the skin.

The biggest fish ever

The whale shark is not only the biggest shark, it is the biggest fish. It can grow to over 40ft (12m) long and even its mouth, which is filled with over 300 teeth, can be almost 5ft (1.5m) wide. Despite its size, it is not as frightening as a great white shark as it is not a predator, and it mostly eats plankton. The species inhabits warm oceans and is thought to have evolved 60 million years ago.

Star of the ocean

The biggest starfish, or sea star, of all 2,000 known species is the Midgardia xandoras, which exceeds 3.3ft (1m), with one example recorded as measuring 4.5ft (1.3m) across.

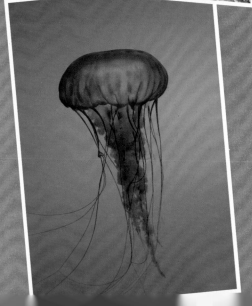

The mysterious giant squid

At over 49ft (15m) long, giant squid are the world's largest invertebrates, both in the sea or on land. But nobody has ever seen one alive. Giant squid have only been seen when they have been washed up on a shore, or caught and killed in fishermen's nets. This occurs mostly in New Zealand and Newfoundland.

The earliest petrol-powered motorcycle

This was designed and built in Germany in 1885, by Gottlieb Daimler and Wilhelm Maybach. It was called a "Reitwagen" – a riding car – and was little more than a push bike with a motor attached; such machines weren't made available to buy until 1894.

Slow it down – to 186mph!

The fastest superbike in the world is the MV Agusta F4 1000, which has a top speed of 200mph (322kph). Manufacturers of superbikes have come to an agreement to put electronic limiters on their top speeds, to keep it to a maximum of 186mph (299kph). This is because they feared competition among brands could lead to too many accidents, and governments would be forced to take action against them.

The fastest blindfold motorcycle ride

In 2003 Billy Baxter took a 1200cc Kawasaki Ninja up to a speed of 164.87mph (265.33kph) with his eyes covered. He performed this stunt at RAF Boscombe Down in Wiltshire, UK.

Largest manufacturer

Japan's Honda Motor Co. Ltd. is the largest engine maker in the world, producing over 14 million internal combustion engines a year. Hero Honda, a joint venture between India's Hero Group and Honda, is the world's largest manufacturer of two wheelers. In 2008, Honda also announced the first electronically-controlled Super Sport motorcycles.

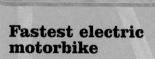

Fastest electric motorbike

This record is held by The KillaCycle, a super-fast electric bike that was built especially for drag racing. In November 2007, the KillaCycle completed 0.25 miles (0.4km) drag-racing course in 7.824sec, reaching a record-breaking top speed of 168mph (270kph).

Earliest automated bike

This was designed and built in the US in 1867 and powered by steam. It was exhibited at circuses and fairs.

The motorbike land speed record

Chris Carr set this record in 2009 reaching 360.91mph (580.83kph) at the Bonneville Salt Flats, Utah, USA.

Longest motorcycle-racing course

At 37.733 miles (60.72km), it is the Snaefell Mountain Course of the Isle of Man TT. It is also the oldest still in use – the first TT was raced in 1907. It is a circuit of public roads that are closed for the race, which is open only to street-legal bikes (they must have silencer, mudguards, and proper seats). The current lap record is 17min 21.99sec, at an average speed of 130.354mph (209.78kph), and was set by John McGuinness during the 2007 race.

Manx racing

Motor racing first came to the Isle of Man in 1904, when the Gordon Bennett car trials were held. In 1998 Joey Dunlop increased his record number of TT wins to 23 with victory in the Lightweight TT.

Paris-Dakar endurance rally

The Dakar, an annual off-road rally, is the toughest test of man and machine, covering dunes, mud, camel grass, rocks, and erg. It was started in 1978 by Thierry Sabine.

Furthest 24-hour non-stop unicycle ride

This record stands at 235.3 miles (378.7km), and was set by Ken Looi in Wellington, New Zealand in 2007.

The world's largest cycle race

The Tour de France, which lasts 23 days and covers over 1,864 miles (3,000km), is the largest cycle race in the world. It was organized in 1903 by a sports newspaper, *L'Auto*, to promote sales, and proved so popular that it was made an annual event. The original plan was for it to last for 35 days, but this proved to be too much because only 15 riders entered; when it was cut to 19 days, a further 60 signed up immediately.

King of bikes

The fastest and most powerful road bike is the Kawasaki Ninja ZX–14, which can accelerate from 0–60 in 2.5sec and produces 200bhp from a 1352cc engine.

Most Tour de France wins

This honor goes to the American, Lance Armstrong. He remained unbeaten in the Tour de France between 1999 and 2005, notching up seven victories.

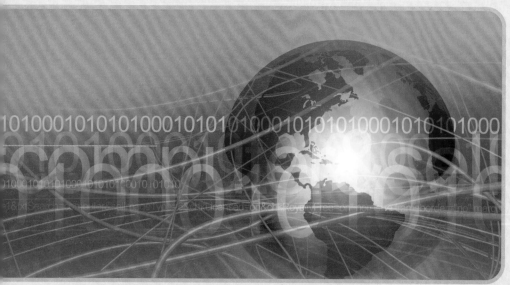

The first global information system

The Internet works by allowing computers to talk to each other via the phones lines; broadband technology meant the fiber optic cables could carry much greater amounts of information. Never before had computers been able to talk to each other in this way before. They can be on at the same time as your telephone – the old dial-up couldn't be – because the cables have enough capacity to carry both signals to the same input point.

First websites

The first website built was at CERN (European Organization for Nuclear Research) and was first put online on 6 August 1991. It provided an explanation about the World Wide Web and how one could set up a web server.

What do they find to write about?

On average, there are 210 billion emails sent every day. That's 2.5 million per second, for around 1.2 billion regular email users. It is believed that around 70 per cent of emails sent are "spam" (unsolicited bulk email). It has been reported that Microsoft founder Bill Gates receives four million emails per year, mostly spam, while Jef Poskanzer, owner of the domain name acme.com, receives a record one million spam emails per day.

The man who invented the Internet

The American Joseph Licklider who was working for the US Department of Defense, and looking for a way to link computers around the country to control radar defense systems, developed the Internet between 1962 and 1965. It began life as the Intergalactic Computer Network, and the first computers connected were at the University of California, Los Angeles, and the Stanford Research Institute, also in California, several miles away.

How much time is spent surfing?

If you have an Internet connection, you probably spend more time on the web than watching TV. A 2010 survey showed Americans spend nearly three hours online via their mobile devices daily. 91% socialize, and 79% are traditional web users.

3hrs
a day spent online via mobile devices in the USA

International gaming

Online gaming was available for the first time at the end of the 1970s and the first of these games was "Mazewar". It is now central to the gaming industry, allowing players all over the world to connect with each other. A report by the company Screen Digest has found that the market value for massively multiplayer online games (MMOGs) in the West hit the $1 billion (£500,000) mark for the first time in 2006.

The biggest map of the world

Google Earth is the biggest map of the world. It can show most of the world's land via satellite pictures in incredible detail.

Virtual golf

The most popular online sport is virtual golf. Standing on a special mat in front of a large screen, the player sees the actual view along fairways of famous golf courses. They swing to strike a rubber peg fixed to the mat, and a computer calculates where their ball would go, taking into account club selection, strength, and angle of the strike, to show the ball's trajectory and landing on the screen. This continues all around the course, and groups of players can link their games via the Internet. Bars in the Japan, UK, and the US, started to install these simulators due to the popularity of virtual golf.

Small beginnings

In August 1994 the sale of a CD in the US represented the first secure Internet shopping transaction. The Internet is a huge global shopping marketplace, and around 27% of the world's population uses it regularly. Developing countries have seen a huge rise in Internet usage over the past few years.

Well-used websites

Yahoo.com is the most used website in the world, while Google is the most successful in the US. Google's search engine generates an amazing $7 billion (£3.5 billion) per year in advertising revenue. Google is named after the mathematical term "googol," which is the largest number possible – a one followed by 100 noughts.

eBay uncovered

Pierre Omidyar, who developed its online trading program, launched eBay in 1995, the world's first online auction and shopping site. Among the first transactions was his girlfriend's trading in Pez dispensers. In 2009, eBay was worth $64.8 billion (£43.6 billion) and owns the most-used Internet banking system, PayPal, and the communications service Skype.

The most popular social networking site

Facebook, founded in 2004, had grown to 200 million active users by the end of 2009. In fact, more than 50 million people signed up in 2009 alone. On average, more than 3.5 billion minutes are spent on Facebook each day.

Priceless food

Truffles and Beluga caviar are both incredibly expensive, but the most expensive food item in the world by far, ounce for ounce, is the spice saffron. It takes about 80,000 flowers (240,000 stigmas) to make a pound of saffron (two football fields' worth

for a kilogram). About 40 hours of experienced labour is needed to pick 150,000 flowers. By the time saffron gets to retail stores, it costs $500–5,000 (£328–3,283) per pound.

Biggest hamburger

The world's largest burger was made at Mallie's Sports Grill and Bar in Southgate, Michigan, USA. It took 8 hours to bake the bun big enough to hold the 185lb (84kg) burger, the enormous meal costing $499 (£328). The previous record-holder in the burger wars, made at Clinton Diner Station in Clinton, New Jersey, weighed 105lb (47.6kg).

Heaviest omelette

The largest omelette the world has ever seen weighed in at an incredible 6,510lb (2,953kg) and was created by The Lung Association, Brockville, Canada, on 11 May 2002.

Largest pizza

Iowa Falls, Iowa, USA, holds the record for the world's largest ever pizza, at 129 x 92ft (39.3 x 28m). Made in 2005, 26 teams converted 4,000lb (1,814kg) of cheese, 700lb (317.5kg) of sauce, and 9,500 sections of crust into a huge pie in the parking lot at Alden High School, Iowa Falls. Donations of $42,000 (£21,000) worth of ingredients were made and more than 200 people volunteered to put together the 50,000-slice pizza.

Biggest stir-fry

The record for the largest stir-fry ever to be cooked was achieved by the Wesvalia High School in Klerksdorp, South Africa, on 22

October 2005. The stir-fry was made on the occasion of the 30th anniversary of the Wesvalia High School and weighed a total of 2,319lb (1,052kg).

Priciest pie on the planet

The world's most expensive pie costs more than $2,000 (£1,000) per slice. Baked in Burnley, Lancashire, in England by Spencer Burge, the head chef at the Fence Gate Inn, it was filled with luxury ingredients. Instead of the traditional steak and mushroom that went in a pie, Burge filled his prize creation with a $1,000 (£500) beef fillet, Chinese mushrooms worth more than $4,000 (£2,000), and truffles. The recipe included two bottles of 1982 Chateau Mouton Rothschild red wine costing more than $8,000 (£4,000), and the pie was topped with gold leaf. The pie was cut into eight slices and the total cost came to $16,390 (£8,195).

Largest sandwich

The record for the largest sandwich ever stands at 8,896lb (4,035kg). The sandwich, 42 x 9ft (13 x 2.8m) and filled with 3,086lb (1,400kg) of vegetables, was cooked up by 160 students at the Ryan International School in Ludhiana, India, in 2008.

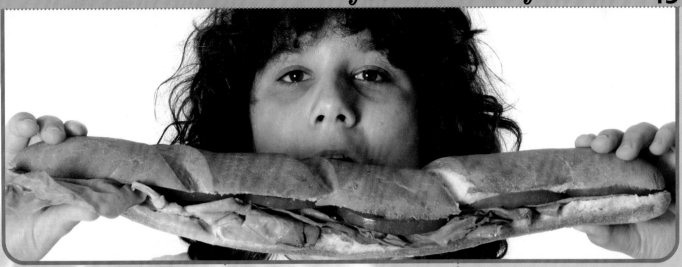

Biggest pancake

Rochdale, in the United Kingdom, holds the record for the world's largest pancake. The pancake weighed over 3ton (3048kg), was 49ft (15m) in diameter and had an estimated two million calories.

It was actually baked in 1994 as part of the 150th anniversary celebrations of the Rochdale Pioneers.

Furthest pizza delivery

In November 2004, Domino's Pizza of Feltham, London, delivered a pizza 10,532 miles (16,950km) away to Melbourne, Australia. Before this, Butler's Pizza of Cape Town had covered 6,861 miles (11,042km), from Cape Town to Sydney.

Rarest wine

Christopher Forbes bought one of the rarest bottles of wine ever sold, for $160,000 (£105,000). It was an

unmarked green glass bottle with the inscription of "1787 Lafitte Th. J." The wine is known as Lafite and is thought to have been owned by US president Thomas Jefferson. The bottle was found behind a wall in Paris, France.

The highest-grossing tour

The Rolling Stones' 2006 Bigger Bang Tour, which took a worldwide total of $609 million (£395 million – inflation adjusted), beating U2's Vertigo Tour that same year, which grossed $402 million (£395 million).

Artists with most UK Number One singles

Elvis Presley leads with 18, closely followed by the Beatles with 17 and Cliff Richard with 14. Madonna has to date had 10 Number One singles in the UK.

The biggest-selling album of all time

This record is held by Michael Jackson's *Thriller* which, since its release in 1982, has sold over 110 million copies worldwide. After Jackson's death in 2009, sales rose again, and songs from *Thriller* helped Jackson become the first

Top of the tops

In the US, The Beatles have spent the longest at the top of the album charts, with a total of 132 weeks and 20 albums hitting the top spot. Elvis Presley is in second with the same number of albums, but his albums have spent a total of 67 weeks at Number One.

741

number of weeks Dark Side of the Moon by Pink Floyd was in the US album charts

artist to sell more than one million song downloads in a week. The first album to top the UK and US charts simultaneously, *Thriller* is the only album to be America's top seller for two years (1983 and 1984); and has spent the most consecutive weeks at Number One (37 weeks) out of 80 on the charts. A quarter of a century after its original release, *Thriller* still sells around 200,000 copies a year, which is more than most albums sell at all.

iTunes record

The billionth download from iTunes – the most successful download music store ever – was Coldplay's "Speed of Sound" in February 2006. The billionth download mark was reached within a mere three years of iTunes' launch.

The best-selling pop single

"Candle In The Wind '97," by Elton John. The record was a new version of his 1974 classic, and was released in memory of Diana, Princess of Wales. "Candle in the Wind" has sold a record 37 million copies worldwide.

Most successful groups

With worldwide sales of 37 million albums and 18 million singles, The Spice Girls are the most successful UK girl group of all time. In the US, Destiny's Child have sold 46 million albums and 15 million singles. Take That are the most successful boy band in the UK with over 33 million album sales. In the US, The Backstreet Boys hold the record, having sold over 100 million albums.

Youngest first-time Number One

Former *Doctor Who* sidekick Billie Piper was the first performer to achieve this in the UK, with "Because We Want To" in 1998 when she was just 15 years 287 days old.

The oldest performer to get a UK Number One

Louis Armstrong, who, at the ripe old age of 66 years 10 months, got there with "What A Wonderful World" in 1968, while Cher became the oldest woman with "Believe" in 1999. She was 52 years 7 months old.

32 ELVIS MARSHALL ISLANDS

Most US Number Ones

In the US, The Beatles have had the most Number One singles: 20. Mariah Carey has 18 and Elvis 17.

Most weeks on the US and UK album charts

In the US, this record goes to Pink Floyd's "Dark Side of the Moon" – 741 weeks, which is just over 14 years. Queen have spent more time on the UK album chart, 1,322 weeks, than any other musical act.

The youngest act to top the UK charts

This was little Jimmy Osmond at the age of 9 years 8 months, with "Long Haired Lover From Liverpool" in 1972. However, the youngest to appear on a Number One single was Jessica Smith, who, at seven months old, was Baby Sun in *The Teletubbies* and it is her giggle that can be heard on their 1997 Number One single "Teletubbies Say Eh-Oh!"

Space mountain

The tallest known mountain in our solar system is Olympus Mons, located on Mars, which is 16.7 miles (27km) high, and three times the elevation of Mount Everest above sea level. The mountain is also 342 miles (550km) in width. On Earth, mountains are formed by volcanic movement, erosion, and disturbances or uplift in the Earth's crust. The Earth's crust is made up of six huge slabs called plates, which fit together like a jigsaw puzzle. When two slabs of the Earth's crust smash into each other the land can be pushed upwards, forming mountains. Many of the greatest mountain ranges of the world have formed because of enormous collisions between continents.

Water sources

More than half of the world's fresh water originates in mountains, and all the world's major rivers are fed from mountain sources. Mountains also cover one-fifth of the Earth's land surface.

Top of the world

Mount Everest, on the Nepalese-Tibetan border, is the world's tallest mountain at 29,028ft (8,848m) and was first successfully climbed in 1953. The second tallest is K2 at 28,251ft (8,611m), in the same Himalayan range as Everest.

High peaks

Outside of Asia, the highest peak in the world is Mount Kilimanjaro in Tanzania, which rises to a height of 19,340ft (5,895om). Oceania's highest peak is Puncak Jaya, New Guinea at 16,535ft (5,040m); Antarctica's is Vinson Massif at 16,066ft (4,897m); Australia's is Kosciusko at 7,310ft (2,228m) and Europe's highest mountain is Elbrus in the Caucasus range in Russia, which stands at 18.510km (5,642m). In North America, Mount McKinley in Alaska holds the record at 20,320ft (6,194m), while Aconcagua in Argentina is the tallest mountain in South America at 22,834ft (6,96om).

Life at the top

The first people to successfully climb Mount Everest were Sir Edmund Hillary and Tenzing Norgay on the South Col Route on 29 May 1953. The first successful attempt by a woman wasn't until 1975, when the Japanese climber Junko Tabei made it to the top, also using the South Col route. The climate changes rapidly at the summit, getting colder the higher the altitude. This is because, as altitude increases, air becomes thinner and is less able to absorb and retain heat. Despite this, the longest stay at the top was Babu Chiri Sherpa, who stayed at the top of Everest for a full 21.5 hours.

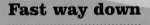

Fatal climbs

K2 was first summitted on 31 July 1954 by a team of Italians, Lino Lacedelli and Achille Compagnoni. Since then there have been over 250 summits (compared with around 2,000 on Everest). In terms of the overall summit/fatality rate of 23 per cent, K2 is the third most deadly mountain in the world after Nanga

Parbat and Annapurna I (both in the Himalayas). Women have also found the challenge of K2 too much: six have reached the top, but, of those, three died on the descent.

Most difficult

The most difficult mountain to climb is the Makalu – an isolated peak with a shape of a four-sided pyramid. It is yet to be climbed in true winter conditions. Lionel Terray and Jean Couzy were the first to climb Makalu, the fifth-highest mountain in the world at 27,824ft (8,481m), on 15 May 1955 as part of a French expedition via the North face and northeast ridge.

First high climb

Annapurna I was the first 26,246ft (8,000m) peak to be climbed. Maurice Herzog and Louis Lachenal, from a French expedition, reached the summit on 3 June 1950. Annapurna is a series of peaks in the Himalayas, a 34 mile (55km) long massif whose highest point, Annapurna I, is the 10th-highest summit in the world.

Fast way down

In May, 2004, Nepalese Sherpa, Pemba Dorje, set a new record for the fastest climb of Mount Everest by reaching the top in a time of 8h 10min. The fastest descent down Everest was by Jean-Marc Boivin of France in 1988, when he made it from the summit to bottom in 11min. He was, however, paragliding. The most dangerous area of the mountain is the Khumbu Ice Fall, where 19 people have died.

Babe Ruth

George Herman Ruth is universally acknowledged as the greatest baseball player ever. In a career that lasted from 1914 to 1935, he batted an average of .342, with 714 home runs and batted in at 2217. He was a good starting pitcher, too, and in a 1916 World Series game pitched 13 scoreless innings, prompting a 14-inning game – both records still stand today. For some reason, he kept a cabbage leaf under his cap and would change it for a fresh one after every two innings.

Cal Ripken Jr

Considered the best shortstop in the history of baseball, during a 20-year career (1981–2001), Cal only ever played for the Baltimore Orioles. He holds the record for playing most consecutive games, at 2,632.

Barry Bonds

Hank Aaron held the record for the most home runs in a career, notching up 755, until Barry Bonds broke it in 2007. He hit 762 home runs, his batting average was .298, had runs battered in (RBI) average of 1,996, and had stolen 514 bases by the end of the 2007 season.

Joe DiMaggio

The only player in baseball history to be selected for the end of season All-Star Team every season he played (1936–1951) was Joe DiMaggio. He achieved a 56-game hitting streak (not being struck out) in 1951 that has still not been equaled. DiMaggio

was also an excellent center fielder, and was famous for his balance and grace of movement.

Most home runs in a season

This record is held by Barry Bonds, who hit 73 home runs in a single season in 2001. Barry holds the records for most home runs in both categories, i.e., for both career (2,558) and season (232 in 2004).

Willie Mays

A genuine all-rounder, who could hit, pitch, throw and run, Willie Mays is tied for the record number of appearances in the All-Star Team (24) and is also fourth in the career home runs list, with 660. Mays was so popular when he played for San Francisco Giants, that 24 May in that city was declared Willie Mays Day. The date was chosen because the San Francisco hero wore number 24 and he was born in May. It also happened to be his name!

Highest career batting average

This record goes to Ty Cobb, who retired from playing in 1921, with a batting average of 367. During the course of his career, Ty, also known as the "Georgia Peach," set an amazing 90 Baseball records.

Diamond stats

The distance between bases on a baseball diamond is 90ft (27m), and the distance from the pitcher's mound to the home plate is 60ft 8in (18.5m); the pitcher's mound should be 18in (45cm) in diameter and no higher than 10in. Many people believe that New York Mets player, Jose Reyes, was the fastest player around the diamond, although there is some controversy over that claim.

The year of change

Although baseball had been a major spectator sport for all of the 20th century in the US, it wasn't until the 1947 season that black players were allowed to sign for Major League teams. Jackie Robinson became the first, when he signed with the Brooklyn Dodgers. Up until that year, black players had played in what were called the "Negro Leagues," which featured some very exciting baseball played before huge crowds.

Most runs in an MLB game

Major League Baseball (MLB) is not always this high-scoring. But the record stands at 49, set when the Chicago Cubs beat the Phillies by 26 to 23, on 25 August 1922.

Earliest around-the-globe expedition

In 1521, Ferdinand Magellan, a Portuguese maritime explorer, became the first person to circumnavigate the globe. Setting

Zoom!

Concorde holds the record for the fastest eastbound and the fastest westbound flights around the world. On 12–13 October 1992, the Air France *Concorde* *F-BTSD* made the westbound journey in 32h 49min 3sec. Then, from 15–16 August 1995, it flew eastbound in a time of 31h 27min 49sec. Both trips required six refuelling stops.

First around the world on foot

The first man to officially walk around the world was Dave Kunst from Minnesota, USA. He made his extraordinary journey from 20 June 1970 to 5 October 1974. About halfway through their trek, in

1924
first around-the-world flight

out from Spain in 1519, he crossed all the meridians of the globe. Magellan started off with 240 crew members, but only 18 survived. Sadly, Ferdinand himself died on the journey, leaving Spaniard Juan Sebastián Elcano to navigate the last leg of the expedition.

Vroom vroom!

In 2005, Nick Sanders made the fastest ever motorcycle circumnavigation in 19 days 3h 25min. He rode for 19,650 miles (31,623.61km). Nick has biked around the globe 20 times!

Two wheels world record

On 15 February 2008, Mark Beaumont, from Scotland, traveled 18,297 miles (29,446.16km) around the globe in 194 days and 17h – on his bicycle.

October 1972, Dave's traveling companion and brother, John, was shot and killed by bandits in Afghanistan. Dave was also shot in the attack, but played dead and managed to survive. He was treated for his injuries in hospital 20 days. After the attack, Dave flew back to his home in Minnesota where he spent another three-and-a-half months recuperating. Then he and another brother, Pete, flew back to the spot where Dave had been killed and completed the last 5,592 miles (9,656km) of his 14,291 mile (23,255km) journey.

Young pilot

In 2007, Barrington Irving, a 23-year-old pilot in a single-engine plane from the US, finished a three-month trip to become the youngest person to fly around the world alone. He finished his journey in 41 days in his *Columbia 400* airplane named Inspiration, which he built from more than $300,000 (£150,000) in donated parts. He traveled 26,800 miles (43,130km) on his around-the-world flight.

Solo sail record

On 23 November 2007, Frenchman Francis Joyon sailed solo around the world in his multi-hull *IDEC II*. It took him an impressive 57 days 13h 34min 6sec.

Hot air

James Stephen "Steve" Fossett completed the first solo non-stop circumnavigation of the globe in a balloon on 4 July 2002 in 14 days 19h 51min.

Who says he's old?

Minoru Saito, a 71-year-old Japanese yachtsman, became the oldest person to successfully finish a solo, non-stop, around-the-world voyage with his yacht, *Shuten-dohji II*, which means "Drunkard's Child". The journey took Saito 234 days and was his seventh circumnavigation of the globe. He broke his own previous record of oldest man to circumnavigate the globe, which he set in 1999 when he was 65 years old.

Round the world

In 1924, the first around-the-world airplane flight took off from Seattle Washington, USA, and, 175 days later, was a success. It had an eight-man crew, including Major Frederick Martin and Sergeant Alva L. Harvey. The trip covered 27,553 miles (44,360km), with stops in 61 cities, and a total flying time of 371h 11min.

The little continent

Oceania is the smallest continent in the world. It is only 3.45 million sq miles (9 million sq km). Almost 3 million sq miles (7.7 sq km) of this is made up of just one country – Australia. The other countries in the continent are New Zealand and the island nations of the South Pacific.

Mad for sheep

There are about 10 times more sheep than people in New Zealand, which is the biggest sheep-to-person ratio you will find anywhere in the world. The entire population of New Zealand, which is made up of two islands called North Island

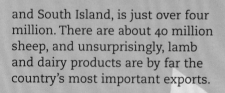

and South Island, is just over four million. There are about 40 million sheep, and unsurprisingly, lamb and dairy products are by far the country's most important exports.

A whole lot of beef

For its geographical size, Australia's population of 21 million is quite small. Much of the country is virtually uninhabitable desert so most people live in cities on the coast. With a population of 4.3 million, Sydney is the biggest city on Oceania, followed by Melbourne, which has 3.8 million people. Australia exports 1.65 million tons (1.5 million metric tonnes) of beef to other countries every year, which is the largest amount exported by any country in the region. The only other country in the world that exports more beef is Brazil.

The oldest peoples

The oldest peoples of Oceania are the Polynesians. Polynesia comprises over 1,000 islands, such as Samoa and Tonga, scattered through the South Pacific. Their cultures can be traced back thousands of years and they are the ancestors of the New Zealand Maoris. The Aborigines are the native people of Australia, where they have been living for up to 50,000 years! Most people in Australia and New Zealand are the descendants of recent, white European settlers.

Record-breaking women

New Zealand women were the first in the world to be given the right to vote. They have been able to vote since 1893, compared to 1918 in the UK and 1919 in the US. Australian women were given voting rights in 1902.

Polynesian inventions

The Polynesian cultures believe that art and inventions are a gift from the underworld. The most famous Polynesian invention that has been taken up by the rest of the world is surfing. The origin of surfing is Polynesian, although this sport became more popular further North, in Hawaii. Explorers' stories, particularly those of England's Captain Cook,

mentioned this sport as far back as 1767; although they lay on the board rather than standing up on it. This was the distant ancestor of surfing and body boarding.

World's busiest arts venue

The most famous building in Oceania is the Sydney Opera House. Danish Architect Jørn Utzon with Ove Arup & Partners designed its distinctive series of pointed white shells. The building opened in 1973, but it was actually designed as part of a competition in 1955. Construction began in 1958, but its design was extremely difficult to build and Utzon resigned from the project in 1966 following a series of arguments. The final result, though, is regarded as one of the masterpieces of modern architecture. Since opening in 1973, Sydney Opera House has become the busiest performing arts center in the world, with over 3,000 events a year and audiences of over two million.

Oceania wildlife

Oceania features many of the planet's record-breaking animals. The Australian koala is the sleepiest marsupial, only waking up for six hours each day, while the Solomon Islands have the most venomous centipede, the Scolopendra subspinipes. Australia's best-known animal is the kangaroo, which isn't naturally found anywhere else in the world.

Most famous mythical bird

In Phoenician mythology – in the 12th century BCE, Phoenicia was a powerful country situated where Lebanon, Syria, and Israel are now – the phoenix symbolized eternal life of their nation. As it reached the end of its 500-year lifespan, this most famous mythical bird, with a

Unicorns

Unicorns feature widely in European myth – the beautiful white horse with a single spiral horn appears as a representation of all things good and pure. Although no physical evidence of unicorns' existence has ever been found, they feature strongly in heraldry, dating back to medieval times. Perhaps the most famous incarnations of the unicorn are on the royal coats of arms for the United Kingdom and for Scotland. The unicorn first became a part of the official seal of Scotland during the reign of King Robert III in the late 1300s.

Gryphons, or griffins

Part of folklore since ancient times, the combination of a lion or big cat and bird of prey symbolizes bravery and ferocity in battle. In Middle

3,700
the age of the oldest dragon found in China

gold tail and beautiful red plumage, was imagined to build its own funeral pyre and sit in the flames. The fire would consume it and a new bird would emerge. The phoenix features in Egyptian, Jewish, and Greek mythology.

Eastern mythology, creatures with the heads, claws, and wings of falcons or eagles on the bodies and legs of lions were made into statues to guard royal residences, and depicted in hunting scenes. By the ninth and tenth centuries in Europe, the griffin was seen as a creature that was at once both human and divine, and features in church architecture as a symbol of Jesus Christ.

Oldest Chinese dragon

Part of popular mythology since the dawn of civilization, dragons are mentioned in the Bible and in ancient Hebrew religious texts. References to dragons are also found in the *Iliad*, the ancient Greek epic poem, believed to have been written in the ninth century BCE. Although depictions of dragons have been very similar throughout time and around the world – reptilian, scaled, yellow-eyed, fire-breathing, and with huge leathery wings – perception of them isn't; in the West, dragons are perceived as monsters and there to be slain, while, in the East, they are far more benevolent and

Centaurs

These creatures had the torso, head, and arms of a man, joined on to a horse's body at the point where a horse's neck should be. Chiron was the only immortal centaur, and was known for his exceptional wisdom. He became the tutor for a number of famous Greek heroes, including Achilles.

The earliest gargoyles

Gargoyles are gutters. Literally. The word comes from the French *gargouille*, which means throat or gullet. They first appeared during the 1200s in

spiritual, and worshiped as a force for good. The oldest Chinese dragon ever found was discovered in the Erlitou relics site in Yanshi City of central China's Henan Province. It is believed to be a 3,700-year-old totem (an object symbolizing family) in the shape of a dragon, and is made up of over 2,000 pieces of turquoise.

medieval times, particularly on cathedrals and churches, as spouts to move rainwater off the roof and keep it away from the walls. They feature as far back as Egypt and ancient Rome, and not all are grotesque – up until the Middle Ages in Europe they depicted animals or holy men.

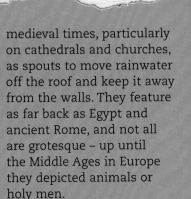

Most vaults over a vaulting horse

The record for the most vaults over a vaulting horse in one hour stands at 5,685, which was set by the Blue Falcons Gymnastic Team of Chelmsford in Essex, UK, in 2003. Ten team members took part, going over the horse over 500 times each, with more than one jump every second!

Most individual Olympic golds

Vera Caslavska-Odlozil of Czechoslovakia has won the most individual Olympic gold

Most World Championships in rhythmic gymnastics

Bulgaria is the king of rhythmic gymnastics, and has won the team gold nine times, between 1969 and 1995. Maria Petrova, a member of the Bulgarian team since 1991, holds the record for the most individual titles – three – and she has never finished lower than seventh in any competition in her entire career.

The most simultaneous handstands

In 2005, in Indianapolis, USA, 1,072 people all managed to stand on their hands at the same time! The record for doing a handstand while walking down stairs is 787 steps. This was set by Russian circus performer Nikolai Novikov in 2004.

Perfect 10

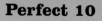

At the age of 14, at the 1976 Montreal Olympics, Romanian gymnast Nadia Comaneci scored a "Perfect 10" on the uneven bars. It was the first time this had happened in Olympic competition, and was such a remarkable feat that the scoreboards were not equipped to display it. As a result, it had to be shown as 1.00! Nadia scored six other 10s at those Games and went on to win gold medals in the balance beam, uneven bars and all-round – no other gymnast has scored so many 10s at one Olympics. Four years later, at the Moscow Olympics in 1980, she also won two gold medals, for balance beam and floor exercise.

medals for gymnastics, with three in 1964 and four in 1968. The most won by a man was by Nikolay Andrianov with seven: one in Munich in 1972; four in Montreal in 1976; and two in Moscow in 1980. Nikolay Andrianov also holds the record for most Olympic medals won by a male competitor – fifteen – in any event.

Most individual Olympic medals

Russian gymnast Larissa Latynina holds the record for the most individual Olympic medals won: 18 (nine gold, five silver, and four bronze), between 1956 and 1954.

The best trampolining

The Federation of International Gymnastics world record for trampolining DD (degree of difficulty) is 17.5, set by Canadian Jason Burnett in 2007. Up until then, a DD of 16.5 or 16.75 was the norm, and the previous record of 17.00 had stood for 20 years. In women's trampolining, the degree of difficulty world record is 15.3, set by Russian Irana Karavaeva in 2005.

Head over heels

American Ashrita Furman holds the world somersault records for distance – 12 miles 390yd, set in 1986 – and speed, with a mile somersaulted in 19min 11sec in 2000. Ashrita holds 21 current world records, including one for pogo-stick jumping all the way up Mount Fuji in Japan. He has set 85 world records during the last 30 years, and even holds the record for the most records held.

Cartwheelin' records

The world record for cartwheels turned in one hour is 1,293 – that's 21 every minute, or one every three seconds – and they were turned by American Don Claps in New York in 2007.

Duration on the Roman rings

Aratak Grigoyan of Armenia set the world record for this, when, in 2003, he held himself in a technically perfect azaryas cross position for 22.9sec.

The most advanced humanoid robot

ASIMO (Advanced Step Innovative Mobility), built by the Honda company in Japan. ASIMO made his first appearance in 1986, and has been continuously developed since then; today's version stands 51in (130cm) tall, weighs 119lb (54kg), and looks much like an astronaut in a space suit. It is the only robot in the world that can run or walk on uneven surfaces, turn, climb stairs, and reach for and grasp objects. It is also the only robotic machine that can understand and react to voice commands, recognize more than one face, and with a camera vision system can avoid moving objects and negotiate obstacles.

Robot jockeys

In Qatar, specially designed robot jockeys ride camels in races, reaching speeds of up to 25mph (40kph).

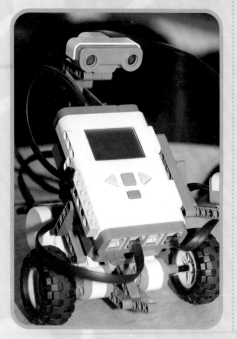

Robot tales

Robots first found their way into popular fiction in the stage play "R.U.R. (Rossum's Universal Robots)," written by Hungarian playwright Karel Capec, and first performed in 1921. 17 years later, in 1938, it became the first science fiction play to be broadcast on BBC television.

Costly toy robot

The most expensive robot is a toy platinum Transformer. It is valued at $250,000 (£125,000) and features a .015 carat diamond in one of the figure's eyes. The manufacturer, Hasbro, wanted it to promote their "robots in disguise".

Work 'bots

Roomba, the housecleaning maid, has one simple function: to vacuum your house. This robot is the first ever built that is designed to live in your home, serve a useful purpose, and be priced for the mass market – at $199 (£100), it costs about the same price as a mid-range vacuum cleaner. You just turn it on and it does the rest.

The fastest robot

The fastest robot ever built is the British built Scuttle – it can cover 82ft (25m) in 6.5sec.

The most articulate robot limb

This honor goes to the snake-like arm made by OC Robotics of Bristol, England, and designed to be used to reach into tightly enclosed spaces in the construction of aircraft. Its robotic arm has no conventional elbow joints and can grip and use tools while turning through 27 degrees, whereas standard robot arms can only turn through six degrees.

The earliest robot designs

These were by Leonardo da Vinci in the 15th century. His studies of anatomy and engineering came together in a series of sketches of an automatic knight. in New York in 1990, it was recreated exactly from his drawings – and worked surprisingly well.

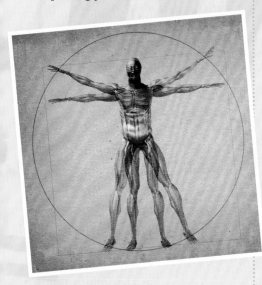

Robot plane

The Global Hawk, a jet-powered aircraft with a wingspan equivalent to a Boeing 737, was the first plane to fly across the Pacific Ocean unmanned. The 8,600-mile (13,840-km) flight, at an altitude of almost 12.5 miles (20km), took 22 hours and set a world record for the furthest a robotic aircraft has flown between two points. It also holds the record for the longest endurance flight by a full-scale unmanned aircraft. It stayed in the air for 33.1 hours.

Film robots

Robots, in various guises, have been the mainstays of all sorts of movies, and in a recent movie magazine poll to determine the most well-known robot, the winner was *Terminator* series 800/Model 101; Hal 9000 (*2001, A Space Odyssey*), and ED 209 (*Robocop*) came second and third, respectively. *Star Wars'* R2 D2 was eleventh, beaten by Evil Bill & Ted from *Bill & Ted's Bogus Journey*, who came eighth.

Longest walk by a robot

This record goes to the Conrell Ranger robot, who set a new record for continuous walking at 5.6 miles (9km), in April 2008.

Meditation helps break the most records

Ashrita Furman holds the world record for the highest number of world records, setting records on 7 continents and over 30 countries. He attributes to meditation his ability to focus single-mindedly on each goal and achieve it. Furman has climbed Mount Fuji on a pogo stick; run 7 miles (11.3km) in Cairo, Egypt, balancing a pool cue on his finger; played 434 games of

17
million – Fonda videos sold

hopscotch in Cancun, Mexico; achieved 9,600 sit-ups in one hour; and played table tennis with an egg.

Science and meditation

Researchers at Harvard, Yale, and the Massachusetts Institute of Technology found, in 2006, the first evidence that meditation can alter the structure of the brain. Brain scans revealed that meditators had an increased thickening in the parts of the brain that deal with control of emotions, attention, and processing sensory input. In the UK, Mindfulness-based Cognitive Therapy (MCBT), which is about 80 per cent meditation, has been approved by the National Institute of Health and Clinical Excellence for use with people who have experienced three or more episodes of depression. Meditation is now offered free for certain patients.

Sleep deprivation

Recommended sleep differs by age but a good night's rest is essential for a healthy body and mind. Sufficient sleep benefits alertness, memory, and problem-solving. In the first year of a baby's life, tired parents lose 400–750 hours of sleep. Sufferers of the rare disease Fatal Familial Insomnia progress into a state of sleeplessness that is untreatable and, ultimately, fatal. The gene that causes this disease has been identified in only 28 families, worldwide.

Go for the burn!

The most popular workout video of all time is *Jane Fonda's Workout*. It has sold more than 17 million copies worldwide – more than any other home video. Fonda went on to release 23 workout videos, five workout books, and 13 audio programs. The actress was responsible for making popular that famous phrase "go for the burn!"

Laughter is the best medicine

The first comedy to win Best Picture at the Oscars was 1934's *It Happened One Night*, followed by Woody Allen's *Annie Hall* in 1977

and John Madden's *Shakespeare in Love* in 1998. Laughing is a great exercise, proven to strengthen the diaphragm and the abdominal muscles. It boosts the immune system, reduces blood pressure and stress, and improves one's all-round wellbeing. Cardiologists at the University of Maryland Medical Center in Baltimore, USA, have linked laughter to a healthy heart. Researchers recommend 15 minutes of laughter a day to help reduce heart disease.

The healthiest nation on earth

According to the World Health Organization, Japan is the healthiest country in the world, where the average healthy life expectancy is 74.5 years. Japan is followed by Australia (73.2), France (73.1), and Sweden (73). The USA, spending more on healthcare per person than any other nation, ranks 24.

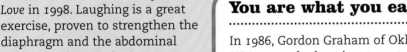

You are what you eat

In 1986, Gordon Graham of Oklahoma, USA, grew the heaviest tomato ever at 7lb 12oz (3.51kg). That's the size of a newborn baby. A tomato is considered a "superfood" – foods that help keep heart disease, cancer, and neurodegenerative disease at bay. Other superfoods include blueberries, broccoli, oranges, pumpkin, salmon, soy, spinach, tea (green or black), tomato, turkey, walnuts, oats, and yogurt.

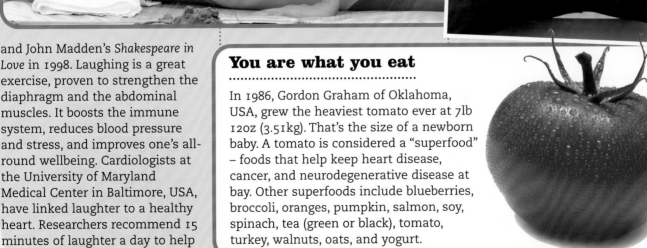

Living the high life

Hollywood actor John Travolta has had a lifelong enthusiasm for aviation, and is the owner of five private jets. These include a customized Boeing 707, three Gulfstream jets, and a Lear Jet. Each aircraft has its own hangar and Travolta has a 1.4 mile (2.25km) private runway on his property in Florida. Travolta's son, who passed away in 2009, was named Jett.

Richest female celebrity

This record is held by the chat show host and global brand Oprah Winfrey, whose net worth is $1,500 million (£750 million). She is also the world's first black female

Wherever he lays his hat

The celebrity with the most expensive property portfolio is P. Diddy (formerly Puff Daddy, or Sean "Puffy" Combs). Among the super-

$3,000,000,000
Steven Spielberg's fortune

rich rapper's homes are a $24.5 million (£12.25 million) mansion on Miami's exclusive Star island; a $5 million (£2.5 million) mansion in New Jersey; a $2.6 million (£1.3 million) estate in Dunwoody, Georgia; an $8 million (£4 million) Manhattan penthouse apartment; a huge house in the exclusive summer resort The Hamptons, in upstate New York, where he welcomes guests to his legendary White Parties; and a ski lodge in the millionaire's playground of Aspen, Colorado.

Most outrageous hotel room demands

Jennifer Lopez's hotel suite must be all white, with white lilies and white roses. White "Diptyque" candles must be prominently placed, along with a special Parisien perfume. Her sheets must be Egyptian cotton with a thread count of at least 250.

billionaire. In second place is Harry Potter creator J. K. Rowling, who is worth $1,000 million (£500 million). The Olsen twins, Mary-Kate and Ashley, are the world's youngest millionaires, with a joint worth of $100 million (£50 million). The oldest female celebrity millionaire is Judge Judy, worth $95 million (£47.5 million).

Mary's millions

Mary J .Blige requests that her performance fee – upwards of $100,000 – is paid to her in crisp new $100 bills. The "Queen of Hip Hop Soul" has received over 26 Grammy nominations, winning eight of them. She received a World Music Legends Award in 2006.

Most famous celebrity zoo

Back in the 1980s, Michael Jackson's best friend was a chimpanzee called Bubbles, who would accompany the singer everywhere, and he also kept a giant python named

Richest male celebrity

Top of the list of millionaire male celebs is Steven Spielberg (over $3 billion/£1.5 billion), followed by DJ Howard Stern. Tom Cruise is the highest-paid actor in the world, and author Dan Brown the richest writer.

500F   2009
MICHAEL JACKSON

Muscles, who he was happy to pose for pictures with. But this was just the start of Jacko's private zoo; once he ensconced himself in Neverland ranch, he built up a collection of pets that included four giraffes, nine parrots, two more giant pythons, two caymans, two anacondas, a male and a female tiger, a llama, and four more chimpanzees. After Jackson fell on hard times, the ranch was sold and the animals distributed to various wildlife sanctuaries in California.

Strangest dress code at a concert

Musician Prince has frequently requested that fans turning up at his shows follow a strict dress code. At his Wembley Arena shows in London, United Kingdom, the pint-sized pop legend told fans they would only be granted admission if they were wearing either pink or peach-colored clothing. As it was, the fans had done their homework and no ticket-holders were turned away.

Most googled celebrity on earth

Michael Jackson's name was keyed into the world's most popular search engine more than any other celebrity in 2009, the year of his death. He was closely followed by Pop singer Lady Gaga and then Country music star Taylor Swift.

Most famous garden in the world

The Hanging Gardens of Babylon is one of the Seven Wonders of the World. They were designed about 2,500 years ago in 600BCE and built by Nebuchadnezzar II, to keep his wife Amytis of Media happy, as she hated the Babylonian desert. The Hanging Gardens were thought to be in Mesopotamia, near what is now Baghdad in Iraq by the Euphrates River. In ancient writings, the Hanging Gardens of Babylon were first described by Berossus, a Chaldean priest who lived in the 4th century BCE.

Deepest canyon

The deepest and longest canyon in North America is the famous Grand Canyon – it is 277 miles (446km) long, up to 18 miles (29km) wide, and more than 6,000ft (1,829m) deep. The Grand Canyon National Park was made a national monument in 1908 and became a national park in 1919. Grand Canyon is also home to 75 different species of mammal, 50 species of reptiles, 25 species of fish, and 300 species of bird.

Rarest star

The rarest aurora in the Northern Lights is the red aurora, like the one of 11 February 1958, which is still talked about today. The Polar Lights (aurora polaris) are a natural phenomenon found in both the northern and southern hemispheres. The Northern Lights, sometimes called by their scientific name, *aurora borealis*, are one of the Seven Natural Wonders of the World. The earliest-known account of the Northern Lights appears to be from a Babylonian clay tablet from observations made by the official astronomers of King Nebuchadnezzar II, 568/567BCE.

Largest wonder

The largest Seventh Wonder of the World, which is still intact, is the Great Pyramid in Giza, Egypt. It stands at 480ft (146m) tall, with a base of 750ft (228m) in each direction. The Pyramids of Ancient Egypt were built as tombs for kings (and queens), and it was a privilege to have a Pyramid tomb. However, this tradition only applied in the Old and Middle Kingdoms. Today, there are more than 93 Pyramids in Egypt and the most famous ones are at Giza.

Roman pride

The most impressive building of the Roman Empire was the Colosseum, the largest ancient amphitheater in the world. Emperor Vespasian started construction on the Colosseum in AD72 but it wasn't completed until AD80, the year after his death. Emperors used the Colosseum to entertain the public with free games, which either lasted for a day or even several days in a row. They usually started with comical acts and displays of exotic animals, and ended with fights to the death between animals and gladiators or between gladiators. The Colosseum was in continuous

300
species of birds in the Grand Canyon

use until AD217, when it was damaged by fire after it was struck by lightning and wasn't restored until AD238.

Largest reef

The largest coral reef in the world is the Great Barrier Reef, which stretches for more than 1,420 miles (2,300km) from near Fraser Island off the coast of Queensland, Australia, to the Papua New Guinean coastline. It is also the only living thing on earth that can be seen from outer space. The waters

of the Great Barrier Reef provide the world's busiest and most varied marine habitats and it is the largest of the world's 552 World Heritage Areas, covering 215,615 miles (347,000km).

The conkers world championship

This is held every October in Ashton, Northamptonshire, UK, with over 300 competitors from 12 different countries as far apart as the USA, the Philippines and South Africa. It is played with untreated conkers only. The reigning champions are: Ady Hurrell (men's); Tina Stone (women's), and the junior champion (under-9) Phillip Broomhead. To win a round of conkers you take three alternate hits at your opponent's conkers. The first one to smash a conker advances to the next round. The world record for breaking conkers is 306 in one hour, held by Irishman Eamonn Dooley, who set it at the 2001 World Conker Championships.

Conquering conkers

The first recorded game of conkers took place on the Isle of Wight, southern England, in 1848. There is specific terminology relating to the game. If you beat one opponent your conker is called a "one-er", two opponents a "two-er", etc. The Isle of Wight game was won by a "5000-er"– it had smashed 5000 opposing conkers.

Hula hooley

The world record for continuously twirling a Hula Hoop between hips and shoulders is 72 hours, set by American Kim Coberly in October 1984. The record for the most hoops twirling at once, for at least three full revolutions and from a dead start is 105, which were twirled by Jim Linlin of China in October 2007.

Largest spinning hula hoop

The largest hula hoop to be successfully spun measured 51.5ft (15.7m) around and with a diameter of 16ft (4.8m). The giant hula hoop was spun by world record-holder Ashrita Furman in June 2007. Ashrita also holds two hopscotch world records: for most games completed in 24 hours – he managed 434 in Mexico in 1998, and in Malaysia in 2006 he finished the fastest ever game at 1min 23sec.

Greatest tiddlywinks player

This honor must go to American Larry Kahn, who, between 1983 and 2003, won the World Singles Tiddlywinks Championship a record 19 times. His compatriot Dave Lockwood is second on the list with 11 wins. Kahn has also won the World Pairs title 13 times, with a variety of different partners.

The longest game of marbles

In February 2006, Australians Jenna and Michael Gray completed a 26-hour marbles marathon to set the world record. The phrase to "knuckle down," meaning to get on with something, comes from the world of marbles: it is said to a player whose turn it is to shoot, as their knuckle has to be on the ground for them to do so.

Most tiddlywinks potted

In February 1966, Allen Astles, a student at the University of Wales, UK, potted 10,000 tiddlywinks in just 3h 51min 41sec, a record-breaking total that still stands today.

The longest, fastest, highest winks

The fastest time for one tiddlywink to be squidged over a mile-long course was set by the UK pairing of James Cullingham and Ed Wynn in 2002, at 52min 10sec. The longest recorded tiddlywink jump stands at

The ancient game of marbles

Marbles has been played since the beginning of civilization on Earth, and the oldest, most valuable examples of marbles are from ancient Egypt, and are around 5,000 years old.

31ft 3in (9.52m), set by Ben Soares of the UK in 1995; and the highest jump is recorded at 11ft 5in (3.49m), which was set by Ed Wynn in 1989.

Rope-skipping world records

The world record for non-stop rope-skipping is 111 double turns in one minute, which was set by

Martin Loenen of the Netherlands in 1997; while American Frank Oliveri, who managed to skip continuously for 31h 46min 41sec in 1989, holds the endurance record.

The biggest skip-in

In October 2006, 50,000 Dutch children and teachers held the biggest skip-in in history. The participants, who came from 335 primary schools around the country, simultaneously skipped for 30 seconds to set a mass-participation record.

The railway in the sky

The Qinghai-Tibet Railway in China is the highest railway in the world, reaching 16,640ft (5,072m) at its highest point.

Largest railway system

The country with the most extensive railway system is the US, even though it is smaller than China and Russia. The US has 140,490 miles (226,097km) of railway track. The USA also has the biggest underground railway system. The New York Subway has a total of 842 miles (1,355km) of track.

The fastest train

In 2003, Japan's JR-MLX01 set the world's current speed record for trains: 361mph (581kph). In 2007, the French railways came close when they accelerated a modified TGV to 356mph (574.8kph). At third place is 320mph (515kph), set in 1990, on a section between Paris and Strasbourg.

Going underground

The very first underground passenger railway system was the London Underground in Britain. Its first section opened in 1863, and ran from Paddington to Farringdon. Today, the Metro system in Moscow, Russia, which opened in 1935, is

887
carriages of the longest model train

A very big miniature train

The longest model train in history was 361ft 10in (110.3m) long. It had three locomotive engines and 887 carriages. The train was put together at Miniature Wunderland in Hamburg, Germany, on 27 November 2005.

busier than the New York Subway and the London Underground. Moscow's network of 180 stations is used by up to 9 million people a day, while Tokyo's twin subway carries close to 8 million passengers every day!

The first trains

The first trains were invented in Britain in the early 19th century, to carry coal. Richard Trevithick (1771–1831) built the very first locomotive in 1804, but George Stephenson (1781–1848), a British engineer, established the first rail network and made trains popular. He and his son Robert Stephenson (1803–59) designed the *Rocket*, which became the model for steam trains throughout the world.

Super trains that float

The fastest train in the world is the Japanese J-R Maglev, which reached a record speed of 361mph (581kph) on 2 December 2003. Maglev is short for magnetic levitation train. The trains do not even touch the track as they float on a magnetic field, so there is no friction to slow them down. The fastest conventional train is a specially adapted French TGV, which reached a speed of 356mph (574.8kph) on 3 April 2007.

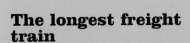

Fastest men on the Underground

On 25 July 2007, relatives Antony, Jamie, Kevin, and Phillip Brown, along with John Stark, broke the record for traveling through every single station on the London

Japanese monorail system

The longest suspended monorail system, where trains run along single tracks supported up in the air above street level, is the Chiba Urban Monorail near Tokyo in Japan. It is 9.45 miles (15.2km) long.

The longest freight train

The longest freight train ever was a BHP Iron Ore freight train, which traveled 171 miles (275km) from the company's mines to Port Hedland in Western Australia on 21 June 2001. The train was an incredible 4.57 miles (7.53km) long. It had 682 cars and needed eight engines to push it along.

Underground network. They took 18h 20min 26sec to visit the 274 stations. In the US, Kevin Foster holds the record for the fastest person to visit every single station on the New York Subway. Foster completed the task in 26h 21min 8sec in 1989.

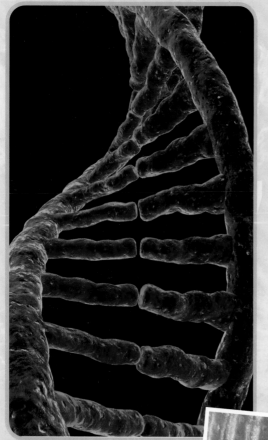

DNA discovered

The full name for DNA is Deoxyribonucleic Acid, and it was first discovered in Switzerland in 1869, but it wasn't until the mid-20th century and research by Americans Rosalind Franklin and James Watson that modern DNA studies took off. Today it is known to be a nucleic acid, and is totally unique to everybody – it contains the "recipe" for the particular construction of every cell in their body. This is why it is so conclusive an aspect of forensic evidence, as our hair, saliva, blood, and dead skin cells will all contain our DNA. When traces of these are left at a crime scene, it is irrefutable proof of who was there.

First known instance of fingerprinting

Chinese traders in the ninth century were the first people to use fingerprinting as a way of authenticating bills of sale and other documents. It wasn't until the 1890s in the West that fingerprints were discovered to be unique, and by 1897 they were included as part of a criminal's record, in India. At the beginning of the 1900s, all police forces were fingerprinting criminals as a matter of course, and using the using them as part of their identification procedures.

Fake!

In 2005 for the first time forensic scientists were able to identify the Turin Shroud, the cloth that supposedly covered the body of Jesus Christ, as fake; it was found to have been produced in the Middle Ages, over 1,000 years after Jesus died.

CSI worldwide

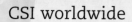

In 2006, CSI: *Miami* broke all viewing records as it was named the most popular program in the world, because it was featured in more country top 10 rankings than any other drama. In 2009, however, the most watched show worldwide was medical drama *House,* with more than 81.8 million viewers in 66 countries.

1869

the year DNA was discovered

It'll never catch on!

In 1886, a scientist called Henry Faulds was the first

Westerner to be able to successfully identify people by studying their fingerprints. Faulds told the UK Metropolitan Police about his discoveries, but they didn't believe it would be of any use to them in their work.

Forensic entomology

The idea of forensic entomology, which refers to the use of insects in post-mortem investigations, dates back to at least the 1300s. Sung Tz'u, a Chinese lawyer and death investigator, wrote a book commonly translated as the Washing Away of Wrongs in AD1247. This book was to be used as a guide for other investigators so they could assess the scene of the crime efficiently.

Digital dabs

Fingerprints are no longer taken with ink on to paper, but by electronic scanning with the hand on a piece of glass.

Identikit

This is the putting together of a recognizable picture of a face, as described by eyewitnesses, to identify a criminal. It used to be achieved by sketching or by using features selected from a series of likely examples. In 1961, Edwin Bush became the first person to be convicted (and executed) with the help of identikit technology. Identikit was replaced by Photo-FIT, a system invented by Jacques Penry, a facial topographer who had been

researching the subject since 1938, before Identikit was developed. In recent times, the most notorious criminal caught thansk to identikit pictures was the Oklahoma bomber, Timothy McVie. More and more police forces are now developing facial recognition software as the next step to fighting crime.

Facial recognition software

This is one of the latest forensic tools. The software has the ability to match faces that have been caught on camera to data banks held on a computer server, and so identify the person concerned. It is becoming increasingly used by border police and to identify people caught on CCTV.

The size of Africa

Africa is three times the size of Europe and is the second largest continent in the world, after Asia. It is 11.6 million sq miles (30 million sq km). The largest country in Africa is Sudan, which is 967,000 sq miles (2.5 million sq km), while the smallest is the Seychelles, which is just 175 sq miles (453 sq km).

African population

Nigeria has the largest population in Africa. With over 154 million people, it is the eighth most populated

country in the world. Ethiopia has over 79 million people, and Egypt over 77 million. Africa is the second most populated continent, with over a billion people living in 61 countries.

Amazing wildlife

Africa has some of the most famous wildlife in the world, such as elephants, lions, and hippopotamus, but it also has some of the most unusual. The lungfish is a fish that can live on land for up to four years; the African giant snail (Achatina fulica) can grow to over 1ft (30.5cm); and coco-de-mer palm trees can live for 350 years. They are all record-breakers.

Two thousand languages!

The most widely spoken language in Africa is Arabic, which is spoken by approximately 175 million people in the continent, mostly in the countries of North Africa. There are about 2,000 different languages spoken in Africa, including over 500 in Nigeria alone. Some African languages, such as Xhosa in South Africa, involve making clicking noises.

The richest and the poorest

Africa has the 25 poorest countries in the world, but some African countries have strong economies. South Africa has the highest gross domestic product (GDP), with $277.5 million (£182.5 million), while the Seychelles, Botswana, Equatorial Guinea, and Gabon all have productive economies.

Natural wonders of the world

Africa is a huge area and home to many of the world's greatest natural wonders. It has the world's largest desert, the Sahara; the world's longest river, the Nile (4,100 miles/6,600km), which runs from Lake Victoria to the Mediterranean Sea; and has Victoria Falls the largest sheet of falling water in the world. Victoria Falls measures 1 mile (1.7km) by 360ft (108m).

Life-saving South Africans

South Africans have come up with some great medical inventions that have saved many lives. The first ever heart transplant was performed by Chris Barnard in Cape Town on 3 December 1967. Allan Cormack, along with the UK's Godfrey Hounsfield, invented the CAT scan which can X-ray soft tissue, transforming how accurately doctors can diagnose an internal illness.

The treasure chest

South Africa holds 27 per cent of the world's gold reserves, more than any other country. The country is also famous for its diamond mines. It is the world's fourth-largest producer. The biggest diamond producer is South Africa's

We are all Africans

Many scientists believe that all humans are descended from Africans, and they were the first humans to roam the land. They think that homo sapiens evolved in Africa 200,000 years ago and migrated to other parts of the world. Africa was the home of many fascinating ancient cultures. The Egyptian culture during the time of the Pharaohs is the most famous, but the Nubians, Carthaginians, and Aksumites were all important, advanced people thousands of years ago.

neighbor, Botswana. Africa contains about 30 per cent of the world's minerals. It also produces large amounts of oil, cocoa, coffee, nuts, and timber.

The greatest

Muhammed Ali is universally considered to be the best boxer

boxing match. In 1978 Ali was defeated by Leon Spinks, but won the rematch, becoming the first heavyweight to win the title three times.

The oldest boxer

The oldest boxer to compete for a world title is Roberto Duran of Panama. On 28 August 1998 he fought, and lost to, 28 year old William Joppy at the age of 47 years, 2 months and 12 days.

Most successful British boxer

Joe Calzaghe (the "Welsh Dragon") has been one of Britain's most successful boxers of the last 50 years. He holds light heavyweight, and super middleweight titles and is also the longest-reigning title holder in any weight class in boxing. He has been WBO super middleweight champion for 10 years and retired an undefeated world champion in February 2009.

Boxing's first million-dollar purse

This was won by Sonny Liston in 1963, when he beat Floyd Patterson.

ever. He gained the heavyweight title twice, after having it stripped from him in 1967 for refusing to fight in the Vietnam War. This forced a two-and-a-half year "retirement". Ali won back the world title in 1974, in Kinshasa, Zaire, in the "Rumble In The Jungle," which is believed by many to be the best ever

The greatest British boxer of recent times

Lennox Lewis was the undisputed world heavyweight champion from 1999 to 2003, during which time he defeated Mike Tyson and Evander Holyfield. His record was: fought 44, won 41, lost 2, and drew 1.

The longest-recorded lightweight title fight

This took place in Nevada, USA, in 1906, before fights had a limited number of rounds. Joe Gans and Oscar Nelson slugged away at each other for 42 rounds, before Gans won when Nelson committed a foul.

The youngest heavyweight champion

This record is held by Mike Tyson (US), who was 20 years and 4 months in 1986, when he beat fellow American Trevor Berbick to become the World Boxing Council champion. After he defeated James "Bone crusher" Smith and Tony Tucker in 1987, Tyson became the first ever heavyweight to hold the WBC, the IBF (International Boxing Federation), and the WBA (World Boxing Association) titles at the same time.

The richest boxing match

This fight took place between Oscar de la Hoya and Floyd Mayweather in 2007, in Las Vegas, raking in $18 million (£9 million) from ticket sales and a further $129 million) (£64.5 million) from pay-per-view. The two fighters are believed to have earned more for those 12 rounds than any other, and although official figures have never been released, de la Hoya and Mayweather are reported to have been paid between $25–45 million (£12.5–22.5 million) each.

The Rock's records

Wrestler-turned-film star Dwayne "The Rock" Johnson, holds the record for most WWF/WWE Championships, winning it seven times between 1998 and 2004. Other titles he has won include: USWA Tag Team Titles with Bret Sawyer; WWF Intercontinental Title; WWF Tag Team Titles with Mick Foley; WWF Royal Rumble Winner; WWE Tag Team Titles with Chris Jericho; WCW Heavyweight Title.

The youngest ever WWE champion

This honor goes to Brock Lesnar, who took the title in August 2002, aged 25 years 44 days. To win it he beat "The Rock".

Still Gamin'

The Game Boy was launched in 1989, and since then it and the Game Boy Color have sold a record-breaking 120 million units. Its most popular game is Tetris, which has sold over 33 million copies, more than any other game for hand-held consoles.

The best-selling digital audio player

This was Apple's iPod, launched in October 2001. The worldwide combined sales of the four models – the Nano, the Shuffle, the Classic, and the Touch – has now passed the 240 million mark as of January 2010, making it the best-selling MP3 player on the market.

The world's smallest cell phone

This record is held by the Xun Chi 138 HP phone, which operates on the GSM network. It has an LCD touch screen, is a mere 67mm in length and weighs just 55 grams, yet it has both a built-in MP3 player and a 1.3 mega pixel camera.

Format wars

Betamax was the first to launch a mass-market VCR (Video Cassette Recorder) in 1975 and offered a higher quality than its rival VHS which came to market in 1976. But in spite of those advantages, the most popular movies were coming out only on VHS, and as the video rental market was becoming so popular, VHS won. But they were both overtaken by DVD at the start of this century. The DVD battle is between the Blue Ray format and the High Def platform.

120
million Game Boy units sold worldwide

The best-selling games console

The PlayStation 3 console broke UK sales records when more than 165,000 machines sold in the first two days of release in 2007. Microsoft sold 71,000 Xbox 360 consoles during its UK launch weekend, while Nintendo sold 105,000 Wii machines.

At home with the Nokia

With over 200 million units sold worldwide, the Nokia 1100 is the biggest selling cell phone ever.

The first portable electronic calculators

They came on the market in 1970, as the result of technology having advanced to the point that they needed very little power to operate. Solar-powered models followed a few years later.

World's smallest laptop

Currently this record goes to the Eee PC 4G. It has a 7in (17cm) display, runs windows and Linux, operating systems, has 512 MB (DDR2) of memory, and weighs only 2lb (0.92kg).

Increasing digital radio

Sales of digital radios have been growing annually. 2008 saw their biggest percentage increase, with total sales over 2.08m. The first five million milestone was reached after eight years in 2007 but, by November 2009, 10 million units were sold, meaning the second five million was achieved in just 30 months.

The Walkman revolution

In 1979, the Sony Walkman changed the way we listened to music forever. It was the first personal stereo to become a mass-market accessory, and introduced an eager world to the idea of music on the move, listened to on headphones and played on a pocket-sized cassette player. Although it had actually been invented seven years earlier in 1972, Sony made them inexpensive enough for everybody to afford one. The first models played cassettes, and then came the Discman, which played CDs, then MiniDisc player, and more recently the MP3 version. As the format for playing music evolved, so the headphones got smaller and smaller to become the earpieces we have now. Today, the Walkman brand has teamed up with Ericsson to produce Walkman phones.

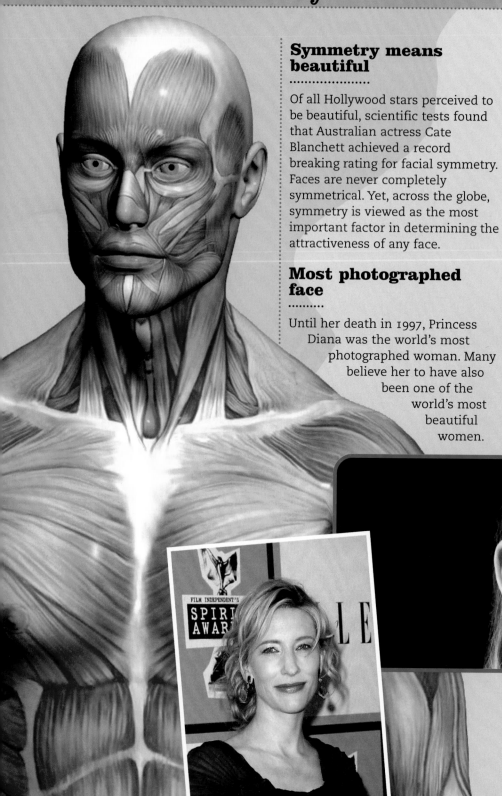

Symmetry means beautiful

Of all Hollywood stars perceived to be beautiful, scientific tests found that Australian actress Cate Blanchett achieved a record breaking rating for facial symmetry. Faces are never completely symmetrical. Yet, across the globe, symmetry is viewed as the most important factor in determining the attractiveness of any face.

Most photographed face

Until her death in 1997, Princess Diana was the world's most photographed woman. Many believe her to have also been one of the world's most beautiful women.

53 muscles in the human face

First face transplant

The first ever full face transplant took place in Amiens, France, in November 2005. Surgeons performed the ground-breaking operation on 38-year-old Isabelle Dinoire of Valenciennes, who had lost her nose, chin, and lips after being savaged in a vicious dog attack. In a controversial five-hour operation, doctors transplanted facial tissue from a donor.

Stick it out

The tongue is the only muscle in the human body that is not attached at both ends. The tongue consists of a group of muscles and most of its surface is covered with taste buds. The tongue is sometimes called the "strongest muscle" in the body but this does not refer to its actual strength. It refers to the strength and power of words.

Face reader

A computer application created to identify and verify people from a video image is called a Facial Recognition System. In January 2001, at the Super Bowl XXXV, in Tampa Bay, Florida, police used a Facial Recognition System for the first time at such a big gathering to search for potential criminals and terrorists at the game. They found 19 people with pending arrest warrants!

Most famous face

Queen Elizabeth II's face has been reproduced more than any other human being. Her face has graced billions of coins, stamps, banknotes, newspapers, and magazines. It's hung in churches, pubs, hospitals, and ships around the world. She is in cinemas, on television, and all over the Internet. Queen Elizabeth II has been the reigning British monarch for over fifty years and is now the longest living monarch.

Who's who?

Bill Choisser, who wrote the world's first book about face blindness and published it on the Internet, is the most famous face blindness sufferer. He once walked right past his own mother on the street! In this rare condition called "Prosopagnosia," you have trouble recognizing faces. A classic case of prosopagnosia is presented in Oliver Sacks' *The Man Who Mistook His Wife for a Hat*. Sufferers find it difficult to keep track of others and, hence, to socialize normally. By two months of age, large areas of the brain are used for face perception.

Faces of the world

The most famous facial reconstruction is that of King Tutankhamun, or King Tut. For the first time, using 3-D CT scans (a series of x-rays of the body at slightly different angles, which a computer then puts together) of the mummy of the "boy king," scientists employed modern technology to paint a virtual portrait of how the young king would have looked the day he died over 3,300 years ago.

Hardest part of the human body

The hardest part of the human body is the white enamel that covers the teeth. This is one of the reasons scientists rely on analysis of teeth to identify fossils. Ninety-six percent of enamel consists of mineral, with water and organic material composing the rest. An adult human has thirty-two teeth and a child has twenty-eight.

Potter's prolific

By playing Harry Potter in all the films, British actor Daniel Radcliffe has starred in five of the Top 20 biggest-earning films.

The most movies

The most prolific well-known actor is Samuel L, Jackson, who in a career that began in 1972, has acted in 88 films. Together these films have taken around $8.5 billion (£4.1 billion) at the box office.

The most successful box office film stars

The record for overall box office success goes to Tom Hanks, Tom Cruise, and Will Smith, in that order. These three are the only actors in Hollywood history to have starred in seven consecutive movies that cost $100 million (£50 million) or more each.

Send for Tom!

According to *Forbes* magazine, Tom Cruise is the "most bankable" actor in Hollywood – this means the one the most people would go to see in a movie, just because they were in it. Second and third on the list are Tom Hanks and Jim Carrey.

81
age of oldest actress to win an Oscar

The highest earning Hollywood film star

This is Johnny Depp, who was paid a total of $92 million (£46m) – including percentages of the profits – for the third *Pirates of the Caribbean* film. Just behind him in second place is Tom Hanks, who can command $74 million (£37 million) per film, followed by Ben Stiller at $38 million (£19.5 million). Nicole Kidman is the highest paid woman on the big screen, with wages of $28 million (£14 million) per film.

The millionaire actor's club

When Jim Carrey starred in *The Cable Guy* in 1996 he was the first actor to be paid $20 million (£10 million) for one film. Now this type of fee is not unusual for a lead actor in a Hollywood blockbuster. Jim Carrey has won Golden Globe awards for his performances in *The Truman Show* (1999) and *Man on the Moon* (2000), and a total of eight MTV awards.

Who needed actors?

When the commercial movie industry got going at the beginning of the 20th century, the people who went before the camera were the least important people on the set – they were usually friends of the director, and had to help move scenery and clear up after a shoot. It was only when the paying public started recognizing them and asking to see more of their favorites that they were taken seriously – the first real movie stars being Florence Lawrence, Lillian Gish, and Mary Pickford.

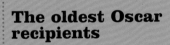

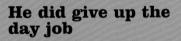

He did give up the day job

You might not know that Harrison Ford is a highly skilled carpenter, and examples of his work can be found in many Hollywood Hills homes. After a brief TV acting career he had returned to carpentry and was building cabinets in George Lucas's home, when the director offered him a part in *American Graffiti*. Lucas later put him in *Star Wars* and influenced Spielberg to cast him as Indiana Jones.

The oldest Oscar recipients

The oldest actress to receive an Academy Award is Jessica Tandy, who won Best Actress for *Driving Miss Daisy* in 1989, aged 81. The oldest actor is Henry Fonda, who was 76 when he won the Best Actor Oscar for *On Golden Pond* in 1981.

Cleopatra's fortune

Elizabeth Taylor holds the record for being the first actress to be paid $1,000,000 when she took the title role in *Cleopatra* in 1963. Elizabeth Taylor has won two Best Actress Academy Awards, for *Butterfield 8* in 1960, and for *Who's Afraid of Virginia Woolf* in 1966, as well as three Golden Globes.

Underground caves

The world's largest cave chamber is Lubang Nasib Bagus (Good Luck Cave) in Sarawak, Malaysia. It is 2,300ft (701m) long, 1,300ft (396m) wide, and at least 230ft (70m) high. Caves form due to natural, geologic processes, like water erosion and tectonic plate movement. Most are formed out of limestone. Speleology is the scientific study of caves.

Deepest cave

The deepest known cave in the world is the Voronya Cave in Abkhazia, Georgia. In 2007, an expedition found the deepest point of the cave to be 7,188ft (2,191m). Voronya Cave means "Crows' Cave." The deepest individual vertical drop in a cave is 1,978ft (603m) in the Vrtoglavica cave in Slovenia.

Largest stalactite/stalagmite

The world's largest stalactite is 105ft (32m) and is joined to a stalagmite to make a central column in the Hall of the Cataclysm in the caves of Nerja, Malaga. Local boys chasing bats discovered the caves in 1959 and it's estimated that the caves were inhabited between 20,000 and 1,800BCE.

Underground, overground

PATH, in Toronto, Canada, is North America's largest underground pedestrian system. With a 16.77 mile (27km) network of underground pedestrian tunnels, PATH connects the world's largest underground shopping complex covering 4 million sq feet (371,600 sq meters), 50 office towers, five subway stations, two major department stores, six hotels, and a railway terminal. It also has 20 parking garages. Once a year, the 1,200 shops host the world's largest underground sidewalk sale!

Largest underground city

The underground cities of Cappadocia in Turkey were once home to 20,000 people in 5th century BCE, making it the world's largest underground city. It is difficult to accurately define Cappadocia's size but it is now believed to be 248 miles (400km) east to west and 124 miles (200km) north to south. The Cappadocians built their 18-storey underground city to give themselves protection. To make it extra secure, its massive circular doors roll across the entryways and seal from the inside.

Longest cave system

Mammoth Cave in Kentucky, USA holds the title for greatest total length of passage at 367 miles (591km). It's unlikely that Mammoth will ever be surpassed, as the second longest cave, the Jewel Cave in South Dakota comes in at a measly 140 miles (225km). Mammoth Cave has 336 miles (541km) of underground caves that have been explored and charted. Over 200 species of animals live in Mammoth Cave. Apart from the usual cave dwellers of bats and mice, Mammoth Cave houses many rare species, like eyeless fish and white spiders. As a result of adapting to the dark cave conditions, many species have lost coloration and become white.

Underground transport

Opening to the public on 10 January 1863, the London Underground is the oldest rapid transit system in the world. Tunnels and transport have long been useful however. In the 19th century, black slaves in the United States were transported to freedom in the North on an informal network of secret routes and safe houses known as the Underground Railroad. Harriet Tubman, a heroine of this era, made 19 trips back to the South and helped free over 300 people.

Deepest cavers

In 2007, the Ukrainian Speleological Association – with 56 members from Ukraine, Russia, Moldova, Britain, Belorussia and Iran – set a new depth record for caving. The team traveled 7,185ft (2,190m) underground, passing the elusive 2,000-m mark at Krubera-Voronja Cave, the world's deepest known cave. Incidentally, "Spelunking" is a US term for the recreational exploration of caves. However, it began to imply inexperience. Most Cave explorers prefer to be called "cavers." "Potholes" is a British term given to predominantly vertical caves. "Potholing" is viewed as an extreme version of spelunking.

Monopoly records

Over 250 million Monopoly sets have been sold worldwide and in 26 different languages. The costliest was produced for the 1988 World Championship and was made with diamonds, rubies and gold and cost nearly $2 million! The longest ever non-stop Monopoly game played was 1,680 hours (70 days) which is over two months.

The most Monopolies

Waddington's produced the first board game with locations from London substituted for the original Atlantic City properties, under licence, in 1936. There are literally hundreds of different versions of Monopoly around the world, with the most popular being based on different cities, sporting teams – Arsenal, Dallas Cowboys, LA Lakers etc – or TV shows or films. There are boards based on *Sesame Street*, *The Simpsons*, *Batman* and *Mickey Mouse*. There is even a DIY set with blank spaces on the board for you to put in whatever you like.

In the beginning there was Go!

The earliest form of Monopoly can be traced back to a game called The Landlords' Game, invented in 1904 by one Elizabeth Phillips, as a way of explaining America's new land tax. It was in the shops a few years later. By the 1930s it had evolved

into Monopoly, and after some development the game was licensed in the UK by Waddington's, who sent it to British prisoners of war captured in WWII. Hidden in each set were maps, compasses, money, and other items to assist escape.

The beginnings of backgammon

Backgammon evolved from two games dating back 5,000 years: senet, played in Egypt, and the Royal Game of Ur, played in Mesopotamia. Both involved dice and a number of counters moved tactically around a board.

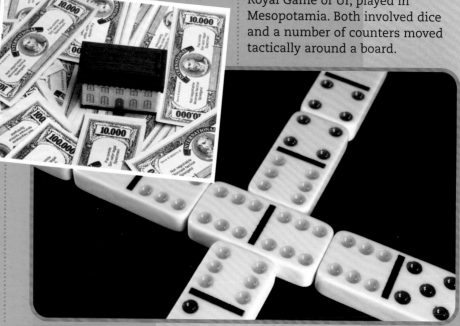

Games of dominoes

The record for the most people to simultaneously play dominoes is 278, set in March 2008 in Miami, Florida, USA.

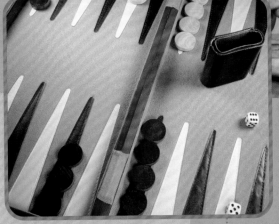

Make it quick

The shortest possible game of chess, to checkmate, is three moves. The shortest Masters game was in Paris, 1924, when Amédée Gibaud of France beat countryman Frédéric Lazard in four moves.

The most chess games played

Hungarian Susan Polgar holds this record, for playing 1,131 games in 17 hours. A former Women's World Chess Champion, Polgar also holds the world record for the most games played at once – she took on 326 opponents in a single run (won 309, drew 14, lost 3), and the most world titles won – four.

The biggest backgammon game

This record-breaking game took place in April 2008, at the Backgammon Masters Freeroll Tournament. Two players tossed cubic meter-sized dice out of a helicopter on to an acre-sized board, where helpers on the ground moved counters that were a meter in diameter.

Longest game of chess

The longest tournament game under modern rules had 269 moves and lasted 20hrs, 15 mins. It was played between Ivan Nikolic and Goran Arsovic in Yugoslavia in 1989.

The most games of scrabble

In Singapore in 2006, 521 simultaneous games of scrabble were played in one place.

Set 'em up to knock 'em down

The world record for domino toppling currently stands at 4,079,381, set on Domino Day 2006 (November 17). The line of 4.4 million dominoes took a year to design and a team of 90 builders two months to lay out.

Fastest crash survivor

Briton Donald Campbell (1921–67) survived a car crash at 360mph (579kph) while trying to break the land speed record in September 1960. He was not so lucky in 1967 when he died while trying to break the water-speed record.

Safest seat on a plane

The worst single air crash was Japan Airlines Flight 123, which crashed on a flight from Tokyo to Osaka on 12 August 1985, killing 520 out of 524 passengers. All the survivors were female, and were seated towards the rear of the plane.

The great Antarctic survivor

The crew of the *Endurance*, led by Sir Ernest Shackleton, had to survive for 22 months in the Antarctic without support (the first time this had ever been done), before they were rescued. The 28 men set off in their ship in 1914 to go on a mission to cross the Antarctic by foot, but the ship got trapped in the ice and was damaged. Shackleton led his men to Elephant Island before he and five others trekked the long 800 miles (1,287km) across the frozen ocean to find help at a whaling station. He returned with a ship to rescue the other men. All of them survived.

638

assassination attempts survived by Fidel Castro

The Titanic survivor

The sinking of the *Titanic* is one of the most famous disasters ever. The luxury liner sank on its maiden voyage when it hit an iceberg on 14 April 1912. A total of 1,517 died, but 706 survived. The youngest survivor was a 9-week-old baby girl, Millvina Dean. Incredibly, she lived to the age of 97, going on to become the last and oldest survivor at the time of her death in 2009, in Southampton, UK.

Lightning strikes

American park ranger Roy C. Sullivan survived being struck by lightning a record-breaking seven times in his life. He was first struck by lightning in 1942, losing the nail on his big toe as a result, and was struck a further six times between 1969 and 1977, but only ever suffered minor injuries.

Assassination attempts

Cuban leader Fidel Castro (b. 1926) is a particularly difficult man to kill. His bodyguard Fabian Escalante claims that Castro has survived 638 assassination attempts, mostly by the American CIA. A communist revolutionary, Castro was in charge of Cuba from January 1959 until his retirement in February 2008. Attempts on his life have included an exploding cigar, a shooting, an infected scuba-diving suit, and numerous efforts to poison him.

Adrift at sea

Captain Oguri Jukichi and his sailor Otokichi were adrift at sea for 484 days after his boat was damaged near the coast of Japan in October 1813. They drifted all the way to the coast of California, USA, where they were rescued on 24 March 1815. It is thought to be the longest time anyone has ever spent adrift at sea. In August 2006, three Mexican fishermen were found in American waters, having spent 9 months and 9 days lost at sea, in a 29-foot boat.

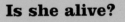

Is she alive?

The quickest way for doctors to tell if a patient is alive or dead is to check their pulse. However, Julie Mills from the UK managed to survive an extraordinary three days without a pulse in 1998. On 14 August of that year, she was diagnosed as dying from heart failure but doctors at the John Radcliffe Hospital in Oxford used a pump to make her blood flow while she recovered.

The beginnings of Western civilization

Greek civilization started in about 1100BCE. A series of city-states developed in Greece before they began colonizing the coasts of the Mediterranean and Caspian seas. The Romans conquered the Greeks in 146BCE. However, the Romans admired the Ancient Greek way of life and Rome was influenced by Greek thinkers, architects, and sculptors. Greece is traditionally regarded as the birthplace of Western civilization and democracy

The first democracy

Cleisthenes, a Greek aristocrat, established the world's first ever democracy in Athens around 500BCE. Only about 5,000 citizens could vote. This excluded most of the population, including all women, slaves, and people who were not originally of Athenian descent.

The undefeated leader

Alexander the Great (356–323BCE) was one of the greatest military commanders in history. Against overwhelming odds, he led his army to victories across the Persian

The greatest empire

The Roman Empire was the greatest in the world. By the time the Empire was officially established in 27BCE, the city of Rome, which was founded in 753BCE, had already taken over all of Italy and controlled the Mediterranean. At its height, the Empire included almost the whole of Europe, most of the Middle East, and North Africa.

50,000
people in Rome's largest amphitheater

and Greek figures such as Socrates and Plato helped determine the patterns of democratic society. They loved storytelling and invented the first formal theaters as well as the Greek myths, which still influence the arts today. They also established the Olympic Games in the 8th century BCE.

territories of Asia Minor, Syria, and Egypt without suffering a single defeat. The king of Macedonia, leader of the Greeks, overlord of Asia Minor, and pharaoh of Egypt, Alexander became the youngest Great King of Persia at the age of 25. He was still only 32 when he died in Babylon.

The most efficient army

The Roman Army was made up of men from all over the Empire. These men were the world's first professional soldiers as their only job was to fight and defend Rome. At first, only property owners could serve in the army, but from the 1st century BCE onwards anybody could join up. These soldiers were required to stay in the army for at least 25 years.

The great Roman theater

The Colosseum or Coliseum is an elliptical amphitheater in the centre of the city of Rome, the largest ever built in the Roman Empire. Originally capable of seating around 50,000 spectators, the Colosseum was used for gladiatorial contests and public spectacles. Such events were occasionally on a huge scale; Trajan is said to have celebrated his victories in Dacia in 107 with contests involving 11,000 animals and 10,000 gladiators over the course of 123 days.

Roman influence

The influence of Rome is still felt in almost every society in the world. Most Western languages, including English, French,

First waste system

The Romans invented the world's most efficient sewage system. Towns and forts had underground drains for dirty water and sewage. The Romans flushed away the sewage with water from their baths so their towns did not smell too much.

Building strength

The Romans invented concrete, which meant that they could build much bigger buildings than anyone could have done before. They also liked to use arches rather than columns, which made their buildings very strong.

Spanish, and Portuguese are based on Latin, the language of the Romans. The Romans were an exceptionally cultured people and had a type of democratic republic until it became an empire with just one leader in 27BCE. Modern legal systems and architecture continue to be influenced by Roman ideals.

The first pet in space

Laika, a Russian dog, was the first pet in space, being sent up in the *Sputnik 2* in November 1957. In fact she was the first of all living creatures, including humans, to be sent into space. Unfortunately, she died from overheating, but she led the way for human spaceflight because scientists were able to tell what they would need to do in order to protect astronauts.

Most unusual pet

Would you want a hissing cockroach for a pet? The Madagascar hissing cockroach is not as fierce as it sounds and is becoming an increasingly popular household pet. It grows up to 3in (7.6cm) long and is a surprisingly clean, docile, and harmless creature. It is flightless and can live for up to 5 years in captivity.

The most famous animal film star

Celebrating its 100th year of publishing, *Variety's* list of top 100 film icons of all time had only one animal – Lassie. One of only three animals to have a star on the Hollywood Walk of Fame, Lassie has had her shows aired in over 100 countries since *Lassie Come Home* in 1943. The character had always been played by one of the original Lassie's descendents until 2006, when British quarantine restrictions meant another collie had to be used.

Fastest pet cat

The fastest breed of domestic cat in the world is the Egyptian mau, which can run at speeds of up to 30mph (48kph). It is also the only naturally bred domestic cat that has spots on its coat, so it has quite a lot in common with a cheetah, which is the fastest feline of all.

Biggest breeders

The largest breeder of working dogs in the world is Britain's Guide Dogs for the Blind Association. It breeds over 1,200 puppies every year and trains them to be guide dogs, also known as seeing-eye dogs, to help visually impaired people. The first guide dogs in Britain were German shepherds called Folly, Judy, and Meta, which started work in 1931, but the most popular breed now is a Labrador retriever.

Australians love their pets

Approximately 70 percent of all Australian households own at least one pet, making Australia the country with the highest rate of pet ownership per household in the world.

Pet goats and sheep

Record numbers of goats and sheep are being kept as pets or companions. They are easy to handle and respond well to human attention. However, the dog is still the most popular pet throughout the world, closely followed by the domestic cat.

The great big barker

The largest breed of dog is the Irish wolfhound. They are consistently up to about 33–36in (84–91cm) tall and weigh

100–125lbs (45–57kg). Zorba, an English mastiff, had the greatest weight ever recorded, standing 37in (94cm) at the shoulder, and weighing over 343 lbs (156kg) – the size of a small donkey.

The oldest feline mother

This record goes to Kitty, owned by George Johnstone of Staffordshire, UK. Kitty gave birth to two kittens at the ripe old age of 30, and, during her lifetime, produced a total of 218 kittens.

The largest pet litter

On 7 August 1970, a four-year-old Burmese cat by the name of Tarawood Antigone, who was owned by Valerie Gane of Oxfordshire, UK, gave birth to a record-breaking 19 kittens. The surviving 15 kittens consisted of one female and 14 males.

30
age of oldest cat to give birth

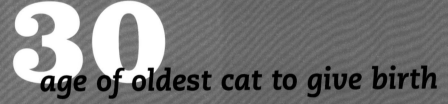

ordered – Watson was sliding his pieces of cardboard around on a table and stumbled upon an amazing discovery. The larger two-ring nucleobases could be paired with the smaller one-ring nucleobases and within these base pairs was the key to the structure and function of DNA.

is named after the 19th-century French chemist who discovered it. Pasteur was a leading scientist in the field of germ prevention. He worked out that germs were airborne rather than internally produced and devised many ways of preventing infection. He also developed methods for vaccination and immunization that involved introducing very low levels of the disease into the system in order to create antibodies within it.

Galileo Galilei

This 17th-century Italian physicist, mathematician, and astronomer developed the first telescope to achieve magnifications of x32. Previously they had been x3 at the most. Galilei vastly advanced the field of observational astronomy. He discovered Jupiter's moons, which have since been named Galilean Satellites, and made other discoveries about the Solar System and how it related to the Earth and the sun.

James Watson

In the early 1960s, Watson made the breakthrough discovery that unlocked the secret of DNA. While using a home-made model of a DNA molecule – he couldn't wait for the workshop to deliver the one he had

Louis Pasteur

To pasteurize milk is to make it germ-free. The word "pasteurize"

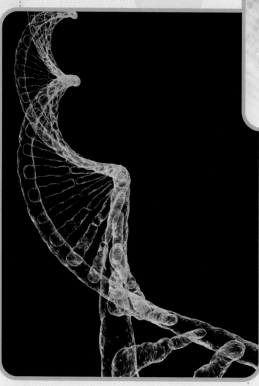

John Logie Baird

Although he didn't actually invent the technology itself, Scottish electronics engineer John Logie Baird advanced the findings to pioneer the first working television transmission system in 1924. His first transmissions were simply silhouettes of his fingers wiggling. In 1927 Baird undertook the first long-distance broadcast by sending a signal over the telephone wires, and repeated the feat across the transatlantic lines in 1928. Between 1929 and 1932, the BBC broadcast TV programs using transmitters Baird had designed. He also invented a very early video recording device – in 1928 – which operated on 78 audio record technologies. The device was called Phonovision, but it was never developed as a commercial product.

1990
the year the World Wide Web was invented

Stephen Hawking

Hawking wrote the most successful popular science book on cosmology – *A Brief History of Time* – which was on the *Sunday Times* bestseller list for 237 weeks, a record for a book on a subject of this nature. Hawking is well known for explaining complicated scientific theories about relativity, the Universe, and black holes in simple terms.

Michael Faraday

Faraday was one of the most influential physicists of modern times, due to his pioneering work with electromagnetic fields. In 1831 Faraday discovered electromagnetic induction, the principle behind the electric generator – a device that converts mechanical energy to electrical energy.

Albert Einstein

Einstein was the first person to unravel many of the indisputable laws of physics and simplify them in a way that could be readily understood. His work on the theories of relativity, gravity, and electromagnetization won him the Nobel Prize for Physics in 1921. He is probably history's most famous scientist, so well known his name is used as a term for genius.

Sir Tim Berners-Lee

Together with Robert Calliau, Berners-Lee invented the World Wide Web in 1990, as a method of sharing information with other researchers, using hypertext. He also built the first Web server, called "http" – Hyper Text Transfer Protocol Daemon.

Seven sixes

Japan's Midori Ito set the world record for individual figure skating when she scored seven sixes at the World Women's Championship in Paris in 1989. With this she equaled the men's record, set by Canadian Donald Jackson in World Men's Championships in Prague, now in the Czech Republic, in 1962.

2006 Winter Olympics, they had won five European Championships in a row, two Grand Prix, two Skate Canada Championships and, in the 2005/2006 season, all five major competitions they entered.

The world's most famous toboggan run

The Cresta Run in St Moritz, Switzerland, which opened in 1855, and is a natural ice run of 3,976ft (1,212m), with a drop of 514ft (156m) and gradients varying from 1:8.7 to 1:2.8. The current record for speed on the Cresta Run stands at 41.02sec, held by Johannes Badrutt, who averaged over 53mph (85kph), finishing at nearly 80mph (128kph).

The fastest skater on earth

The world's fastest skater is Canadian Jeremy Witherspoon, who covered 500m in 34.63sec, at a speed of 14.44m/sec.

Chain of ice skaters

The longest chain of ice skaters is 225. The record was set by a chain of children aged between 8 and 15, in Mexico City in January 2008.

Ice hockey nation

The most successful ice hockey nation is Canada, who have won 37 medals at 22 different Winter Olympics (11 of them gold). Behind them are the former Soviet Union, with 7 out of 9 gold medals; and the USA, with 13 medals, three of them gold.

Best free skaters

Russians Tatiana Totmianina and Maxim Marinin are considered to be the best free skating couple ever to grace the ice. Before they gave up their amateur status following the

The fastest people on skis

The men's World Speed Skiing champion is Italian Simone Origone, who reached 156mph (251.4 kph) at Les Arcs, France, in 2006. The women's champion is Swede Sanna Tidstrand who achieved 151mph (242.59kph) at the same meeting.

The longest ever ski jump

Norwegian Bjorn Romoren ski-jumped 784ft (239m) in Planica, Slovenia, in 2005. At that meeting, Janne Ahonen from Finland actually covered a distance of 787ft (240m), but because he fell over when he landed the record didn't count.

Best National Hockey League (NHL) team

This record goes to the Montreal Canadiens, who have triumphed in the Stanley Cup (the NHL Championship) 24 times. This makes them the most successful national ice hockey team in history.

Oldest hockey trophy

The NHL's Stanley Cup is the oldest still-contested sporting trophy in the US. It started in 1893.

Non-stop skiing

The world record for a 24-hour skiing event is held by Eric Sullivan of the USA who covered 34 laps of a course to record a distance of 51,068ft (15,500m); the women's record is held by Molly Zurn of the USA who managed 22 laps of the same track to record a distance of 33,041oft (10,000m).

Ice cricket

England are the World Ice Cricket champions, after Brighton & Hove Cricket Club won the 2008 Ice Cricket World Cup by beating fellow Englishmen Drovers CC. The championship was held on a frozen lake in Riga, Latvia.

Ice golf

Golf has been played on ice since the 17th century, as can be seen in paintings from that time. The World Ice Golf Championship has been held in Greenland

since 1997. It is played with a red ball, on a nine-hole course, with the greens and fairways smoothed off. The holes are twice the diameter of regular golf holes. Temperatures can get as low as -50 °C (-58 °F) and there may well be hazards such as polar bears or albatrosses.

cardiovascular system but does not force them to exhaustion. Long-distance running, jogging, biking, rock-climbing, and swimming are all endurance sports.

Fastest marathon

On 28 September 2008, Haile Gebrselassie of Ethiopia set the fastest male time for a marathon, at 2h, 3min, 59sec. The fastest female time was set by Paula Radcliffe of Great Britain on 13 April 2003 at 2h, 15min, 25sec. For hardcore endurance athletes, an UltraMarathon is 134 miles (215km) while an "Ekiden" is a 316 miles (508km) relay race. More than 500 marathons are organized annually worldwide.

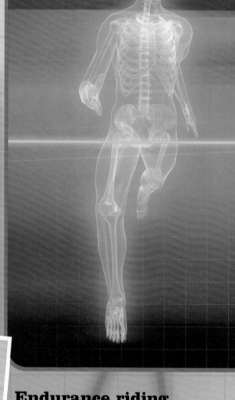

What is stamina?

The most popular endurance test is the marathon, a long-distance running event with an official distance of 26.2 miles (42.195km). To run the marathon you need stamina, or endurance. Endurance training tires the muscles and

Endurance riding

"Endurance riding" refers to long distance races by a one horse-rider pair. The Tevis Cup is a famous 100-mile (160-km), 24-hour endurance race across the Sierra Nevada in the Western United States. The quickest ever time was 10h, 46min by Boyd Zontelli in 1981.

Hereditary endurance?

In 2007, Professor Kathryn North from the University of Sydney was the first person to make the link between genetics and endurance in athletes. They have a gene that makes their muscle metabolism more efficient, so they are less likely to suffer fatigue. This means that potential endurance athletes might be identified at an early age by analyzing their blood.

Biggest workout

Thailand held one of the world's largest aerobics workout session after nearly 47,000 people joined Prime Minister Thaksin Shinawatra for a one-hour session. It's advised to get at least 20 minutes of aerobic activity three times per week. How quickly you can increase endurance depends on age, gender and general fitness level. Endurance means "over a length of time," and endurance exercise

is cumulative. This means that if you want to increase your endurance from 20 minutes of training to 40 minutes, you don't have to do it all at once. You can do two 20-minute sessions during one day.

Longest aerobics session

The longest aerobics marathon lasted 24 hours and was performed by aerobics trainer Duberney Trujillo of Colombia. The record-breaking session took place in the car park of Olimpica Mall, Dosquebradas, Colombia on 26–27 February 2005. To perform endurance sports, the body goes into an aerobic state. "Aerobic" means requiring air... or oxygen. Aerobic exercise is the opposite to anaerobic exercise, where the muscles are strained very intensely for a short period of time, such as in bodybuilding.

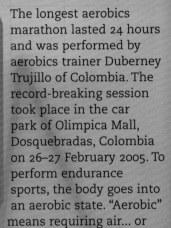

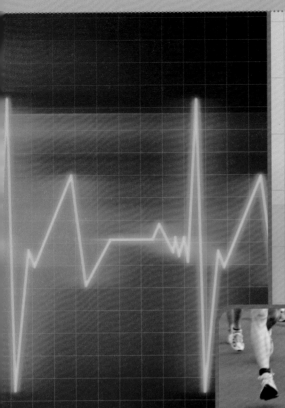

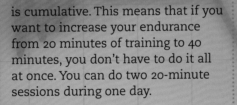

What foods affect endurance?

Marathon runners are famous for eating pasta the night before the race. Carbohydrates provide runners with more energy than any other food group. Without it, they would not have enough energy to finish the race. When the body finishes breaking down the readily accessible glucose, it looks for energy from stored fat. Throughout their activity, long-distance athletes replenish their bodies with fitness bars, bananas, and energy drinks.

Alcohol and endurance

The fastest mixologist in the world is Chris Raph, who set a new world record by pouring 662 delicious cocktails in 60mins in May 2009. Alcohol, even when drunk socially the day before endurance training, depletes your body not only of water, but also essential minerals like potassium and sodium. It negatively impairs your balance, coordination, reaction time, as well as your ability to regulate temperature.

The greatest vocal ranges

American Tim Storms is the record-holder, with a range of six octaves. He has also hit the lowest note, B-2, which is two octaves lower than the lowest B on a piano keyboard. The singer with the largest female range is Georgia Brown. The Brazilian singer has an eight-octave range from G2 to G10.

The biggest, most elaborate production

This honor goes to the musical stage play of *Lord of the Rings*. Opening in 2007, the production costs $60 million (£30 million), and features 17 moveable elevators set into the revolving stage, while the cast of 65 swings out over the audience on harnesses and climbs from balconies. The performance is just under 3 hours long.

The longest running Broadway musical

Andrew Lloyd Weber's opera, *Phantom of the Opera* first opened in 1988 and is still running, over 20 years and over 9,000 performances later. It is the most successful stage event ever put on, with combined earnings from London (where it has run for over 23 years), New York, and other productions around the

989
dancers in world's largest ballet class

The greatest number of consecutive fouettes

This is a pirouette with the leg flicked round to spin, and the record is 38, which was performed by American Leigh Zimmerman in London in 2001, in her role as murderer Velma Kelly in the West End musical *Chicago*.

world of a staggering $3.2 billion (£1.6 billion).

The largest single ballet class

A total of 989 dancers created this record by dancing together at the Canal Walk Shopping Centre in Cape Town, South Africa, in August 2008.

The longest high-kicking chorus line

In Toronto, Canada, in 2006, 1,681 people formed a record chorus line. The participants had to link arms and kick for five minutes without stopping.

The most successful opera singers

This record is held by The Three Tenors – Luciano Pavarotti, Placido Domingo, and Jose Carreras. Before Pavarotti's death in 2007, they gave a series of huge outdoor concerts around the world, often coinciding with the FIFA World Cup – Dodger Stadium in Los Angeles (1994); Champ des Mars in Paris (1998); and Yokohama in Japan (2002). All three shared a passion for football. In their first two concerts, the tenors reached a combined television audience of

World's biggest stage

This is found in the Reno Hilton, Reno, Nevada, US. The stage measures 174ft x 241ft (53.3m by 73.4m) and boasts three elevators and two turntables, each with a diameter of 62ft (19m).

Youngest English conductor

When Alex Prior was 14 years old, he became the first, and youngest, English schoolboy to conduct a performance of his own music for a ballet at Moscow's prestigious New Opera. His adaptation of *The Jungle Book* by Rudyard Kipling was

over two billion people, and combined audio and visual recordings of all three have sold 23 million copies, making them the best-selling classical recordings of all time.

London's longest running stage musical

This is *Les Miserables* in London's West End, which opened in 1985. *Phantom of the Opera* is the second longest running, opening in 1986.

written for a full orchestra. Prior is something of a prodigy, having already laid claim to being the youngest ever conductor of the National Symphony Orchestra at the Barbican in London. When he was 12, he became the youngest commended musician in the BBC's *Young Composer of the Year* competition.

Most rain

The highest ever annual rainfall was at Cherrapunji, India, when 86.8ft (26.4m) fell between August 1860 and July 1861. Rainforests are famous for their high precipitation, hence the term "rain forest". The annual rainfall in the Amazon is around 6.7ft (2.04m). Seattle in Washington, USA, receives only about 3ft (0.91m) of rain annually, as a drizzle over long periods.

The world's largest "pharmacy"

Rainforests are home to two-thirds of all living animal and plant life on Earth. The National Cancer Institute claims 70 per cent of plants and 1,430 varieties of tropical plant with anti-cancer properties are found in the rainforests. Twenty-five per cent of all drugs are also derived from rainforest ingredients.

Disappearing rainforest

In recent years there has been a record drop in rainforest cover: the forests have gone from covering 14 per cent of the Earth's surface to a low of 6 per cent. Experts warn that if we do not slow the rate of rainforest deforestation, they may have disappeared in less than 40 years. Rainforests are often in

developing countries, where the land is perceived as having greater value for its logging, mining, and farming capabilities. Chainsaws, bulldozers, or fires clear the rainforests while farming and ranching operations plough the land. Nearly 1.5 acres (0.6 ha) of rainforest are lost each second.

Missing species

The deforestation process taking place across the world means that we are losing living things at a record-breaking rate. A total of 137 species of plant, animal, and insect are being lost per day. That's 50,000 species a year that we will never learn about.

Tropical forest fires

Due to land-clearing as a result of logging or to make way for plantations, there have been a record number of forest fires. Every year there are more fires, which spread faster and further. In tropical latitudes, months pass without any rain and in the dry season forests become susceptible to fire, but deforestation is making the problem much worse.

Dry forests

The largest areas of tropical dry forest in the world grow in India and the surrounding countries, where monsoon rains occur. Tropical dry forests grow in parts of the tropics where less rain falls.

137
rainforest species lost every day

Amazonian homes

When Christopher Columbus first landed in the Americas in 1492, there were 1.5–2 million indigenous people in the Amazon but now there are around 940,000. It is estimated that this is the smallest number there have ever been, but it difficult to measure accurately. Rainforests home about 50 million of the Earths 250 million indigenous peoples. But most rainforest populations are in severe decline. Three of the larger, well-known tribes are the Pygmies, the Huli, and the Yanomami. Pygmies are some of the shortest people on Earth. The average height of a Pygmy adult is 59in (150cm) or shorter.

No sweat!

People who live in the rainforest sweat less than people in any other habitat in the world. This is because the moisture in the air is so high that sweating is not an efficient way to cool their bodies.

Biohazard

Malaysia and Indonesia produce about 80 per cent of the world's palm-oil biofuel. These are farmed in areas once covered by rainforest. By 2022, 98 per cent of the Malaysian and Indonesia rain forests will be gone.

Earth's lungs

The Amazon Rainforest has been named the "Lungs of the Planet" because it produces nearly 20% of the world's oxygen on its own. No other forest habitat or region in the world produces a bigger percentage. Rainforests absorb carbon dioxide from the air and, in turn, give us fresh, clean oxygen. They act as the Earth's thermostat, regulating temperatures and weather patterns.

Desperate measures

It is estimated that the Democratic Republic of Congo (DRC) is consuming record amounts of ape, monkey, bird, and rodent: about 1.7 million tons (1,000kg) a year. A rapidly growing population combined with harsh economic conditions have rendered many Congolese dependant on what is called bush meat, both as a source of protein and as a source of income.

The Superbowl

The Superbowl dates back to 1967, and is the biggest sporting event of the year in the USA. Played on a Sunday afternoon in late January, it leads to record numbers of flights being canceled because crew want the day off and very few people want to travel while the game is being played.

Superbowl victories

The Pittsburgh Steelers have won the Superbowl a record six times (IX, X, XII, XIV, XL and XLIII) beating the Dallas Cowboys (VI, XII, XXVII, XXVIII, XXX) and San Francisco 49ers (XVI, XIX, XXIII, XXIV, XXIX) who have both won it five times.

The Dallas Cowboys remain the only NFL team to record 20 consecutive winning seasons – 1966–1985 – an NFL record that remains unbroken and unchallenged.

TV audiences

The Superbowl is the most-watched televized event of the year in the USA, with approximately half of the TV sets in the country being tuned in to it. The 2008 game (Superbowl XLII, New York Giants vs. New England Patriots), achieved the second largest audience in US history at 97.5 million. This was beaten only by the last episode of M*A*S*H in 1983.

TV advertising

Advertising on television directly before or during the Superbowl has become the most expensive slot in history. In 2010, the cost of a 30-second commercial was approximately US $3.01 million (£1.96 million). This excludes production costs and fees.

Greatest Superbowl player

Linebacker Charles Haley has the best individual Superbowl record, and is the only player in NFL history to finish on the winning side five times, twice with San Francisco 49ers (XXIII and XXIV) and three times with Dallas Cowboys (XXVII, XXVIII and XXX).

Most successful NFL player

This record goes to San Francisco 49ers quarterback Joe Montana, whose professional career lasted from 1979 to 1994. During that time Montana won the Superbowl four times, was voted the 'bowl's Most Valuable Player three times (XVI, XIX and XXIII), and had the highest passing rate in the league in 1987 and 1989.

Invincible (almost)

When the New England Patriots reached the 2008 Superbowl, they were the first team to win every game of the season since Miami Dolphins in 1972. Even though the season is longer now than it was in 1972. Unfortunately, the Patriots could not match the Dolphins and win the final too, they lost 17–14 to the New York Giants.

only running back to win NFL MVP (Most Valuable Player) and Superbowl MVP in the same year.

Most rushing yards

Running back Emmitt Smith of the Dallas Cowboys holds this record, with 18,355 between 1990 and 2004. He is also the first player in NFL history with 11 consecutive 1,000-yard rushing seasons, including five straight seasons with over 1,400. In 1993 Smith became the

Highest paid NFL players

The highest paid NFL player as of 2009 is Julius Peppers (Carolina Panthers), whose annual salary is $16.63 million (£10.83 million). Giants Quarterback Eli Manning has the most lucrative contract: $97.5 million (£63.47 million) over 6 years.

Most touchdowns in a career

San Francisco 49ers wide receiver Jerry Rice holds this record. He took the ball over the line 209 times between 1985 and 2004.

Most touchdowns in a season

This record goes to LaDainian Thompson, who scored 31 for the San Diego Chargers in 2006.

Royale car rolls

The 2006 James Bond movie *Casino Royale* holds the record for the most car rolls in a film. As part of a car chase scene, an Aston Martin was shot into the air at high speed by a nitrogen-powered cannon and barrel-rolled seven times. The driver was British stuntman Adam Kirley. It took place at Millbrook Proving Ground in Milton Keynes, UK.

Jumping the length of a football pitch

Australian motor cross star Robbie Maddison holds the world record for the longest ever jump on a motorcycle. In March 2008, in the precincts of the Melbourne Docklands, Australia, Maddison bettered his previous record – the length of an American football

Dangerous film stunts

Hong Kong martial arts expert Jackie Chan (1954–) has performed more film stunts than any other actor. He became a stuntman in

408
consecutive upside-down rolls with a plane

pitch – on his Honda CR 500. The bike hit the ramp at over 102.5mph (165kph), to reach a height of over 65.6ft (20m), before landing 352ft (107.29m) away.

1971 for the Bruce Lee film *Fist of Fury* and has gone on to star in over 100 films as an actor. He does all his own stunts, including the most dangerous ones, and has broken many bones. He once fell from a tree, fracturing his skull, when performing a stunt for *Armor of God* (1985). Chan's first major breakthrough was in the 1978 film *Snake in the Eagle's Shadow*.

Ultimate flight control

On 29 January 2007 Hungarian Zoltán Veres rolled his plane upside down 408 consecutive times during an airshow in the United Arab Emirates.

Sub zero champion

In 2010, Wim Hof of the Netherlands, known as the Iceman, set a new record for the longest ice bath when he remained up to his neck in an ice container for 1hr 44min in Tokyo, Japan. In 2009, he completed a full marathon of 26.2miles (42.195km) above the polar circle in Finland in temperatures close to -20°C (13.99°F), in 5hrs 25mins, in only a

pair of shorts and sandals. That same year, he climbed 19,341ft (5,895m) up Mount Kilimanjaro in two days, in a pair of shorts!

Star stuntman

Dar Robinson is widely regarded as the most famous and innovative stuntman of all time. He was the first person to skydive out of a cargo plane at 12,000ft (3,658m) while "driving" a small sports car.

Longest wall of fire

The Marine Corps Air Station in Yuma, Arizona, USA, created the world's longest wall of fire at the Yuma Air Show in March

2009. Using dynamite, electric blasting caps, and 20,000ft (6,096m) of detonation cord, they created a fire wall nearly 10,000ft (3,048m) long with flames reaching up to 131.2ft (40m) high. The previous record was 6,635ft (2,022m) long.

Blindfold speed record

Billy Baxter from Britain holds the world record for the fastest motorcycle speed while wearing a blindfold. The rider, who is actually blind, reached a speed of 164.9mph (265.3kph) on 2 August 2003 at Boscombe Down in Wiltshire, UK, an RAF site.

Moving human pyramid

On 5 July 2001, the Dare Devils Team of the Indian Army Signal Corps managed to form a human pyramid of 201 men riding on the top of 10 motorcycles. The pyramid traveled for 424ft (129m) on the Gowri Shankar Parade Ground in Jabalpur, India.

The size of Europe

Europe is the world's second smallest continent. It is 4 million sq miles (10.4 million sq km) and has a population of over 700 million. Russia is sometimes considered to be Europe's biggest country, but a lot of it is in Asia. In total, it is 6.6 million sq miles (17 million sq km), which makes it the largest country in the world and bigger than the rest of the whole of Europe. Russia's population is 142 million.

London's population explosion

London grew faster than any other city in the world during the Industrial Revolution. It grew from having less than one million people at the beginning of the 19th century to having over 6 million people by the end of it. London became the most populous city in the world in the 1830s until it was surpassed by New York in the 1920s. Its current population is over 8 million, making it the biggest in the European Union.

The city of two continents

Istanbul, the largest city in Turkey, is split between the continents of Asia and Europe. The Bosporus, a strait which runs through the center of Istanbul, is considered to be the dividing line between the two continents. The city's culture reflects this unusual geographical position, with its amazing mix of Western and Eastern-style customs, cuisine, and architecture. If the whole of the city of Istanbul was considered to be in Europe, it would be the continent's most populous city, with over 12 million inhabitants.

The smallest countries

Europe now has over 50 countries, the number recently increased by the break up of Yugoslavia into 7 states. For historical reasons, some cities have become sovereign states, making them the world's smallest countries. Monaco is just 0.75 sq miles (1.95 sq km) and has a population of 33,000. In 1993, Monaco became a member of the UN, with full voting rights. The Vatican City, the home of the Pope, is the smallest independent state in the world: it has a population of about 850 in an area of 0.18 sq miles (0.44 sq km).

8 million people in the largest European city

European wildlife

Minke whales are the most common species of whale found in the Atlantic coasts of Europe and in parts of the Mediterranean. They can be seen all year round, but especially in the summer months. Humpback, Sperm, Fin, and even Beluga whales can also be seen. Killer whales can be found off the cost of Norway, as can seals, one of the whales' main sources of food.

Favorite holiday destinations

The top holiday destination for Europeans is Italy, followed by France, and finally Spain. One quarter of all Americans choose the UK over any other European destination.

Richest Europeans

Liechstenstein is currently the richest country in Europe, followed by Luxembourg, Norway, and Ireland. This is based on Gross Domestic Product (GDP), measured by the amount of goods and services that are produced domestically by a country during the year. Liechstenstein is a constitutional monarchy, while Luxembourg is the world's only remaining sovereign Grand Duchy, a parliamentary democracy headed by a constitutional monarch.

The inventors of Europe

The British are known as a nation of inventors. British inventions include the train, the jet engine, tarmac, the sewing machine, and the rubber band.

The first functioning computer

The ENIAC – Electronic Numerical Integrator And Computer, unveiled in 1944 by the University of Pennsylvania, was 8ft (2.4m) tall, 3ft (0.9m) deep and an astonishing 80ft (24m) long. It weighed just under three tons and cost $500,000 (£254,000). For all of this, it could add, subtract, multiply, and divide 10-digit numbers in under a second. However, that was about all it could do – and it needed six people to operate it.

Smaller and smarter technology

In the 1960s, new transistor technologies meant that computers could become much smaller, use less power, generate less heat, and could be designed to carry out more complex tasks much more reliably than before. By the 1970s, integrated circuitry and the advent of the first commercial microprocessor (the Intel 4004) meant that computers could also have increased capacity in much smaller boxes. The Intel series, in the 1980s, took this to another level and meant that computer technology was now small enough and inexpensive enough to be used in all sorts of everyday items like TVs, washing machines, and cars. The rise of the PC happened at the end of the 1990s, and along with the Internet, is now part of nearly every household.

The first PCs

In 1965, Texas Instruments, who developed the first integrated circuits, needed an application to demonstrate the advantage of their new miniaturizing technology, so developed the "CalTech" prototype pocket calculator, the first patented portable calculator.

The world's most amazing chip

The silicon chip has made computers both inexpensive and small, and so within the reach of nearly everyone. Yet the chip still allows computers to be powerful. Silicon chips plug into circuit boards to allow easy manufacture, upgrade, and repair of computers. Since they are fully-fledged circuits, just shrunk down, they can be used in conjunction with each other to provide the speed and capacity people expect form modern PCs.

Computer versus brain

Your brain is more powerful than any computer. While the average desktop model will can execute approximately 100 million instructions per second, the human

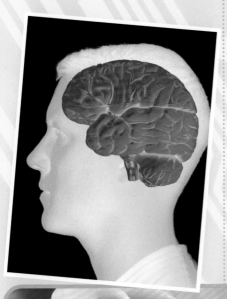

brain is capable of quite easily processing three times that amount of information.

The most powerful computer in the world

This is currently the MD Grape-3, built by the Japanese company RIKEN. The MD Grape-3 is the first computer to perform at petaflops (10 to the power of 15 floating point operations per second) making it three times faster than its nearest rival the BlueGene/L.

The world's smallest hard disk drive

This record goes to the MK1MT, made by Toshiba, which has a 0.85-in (22-mm) diagonal. In other words, it is roughly the size of a postage stamp. It comes with a 4GB or a 2GB capacity and is used in the manufacture of cell phones.

The first hard disk drive

Unveiled by IBM in 1956, the world's first computer hard drive was the size of a walk-in wardrobe, and had a capacity of five megabytes, meaning it handled about as much data as today's smallest MP3 player.

Where do we put them?

In 2009, 80.6% US homes owned a computer. Of these, 91.6% had Internet connection. 2010 marked over 2.5 billion owners worldwide, 1.9 billion with Internet access. The disposing of unwanted computers is a serious environmental issue.

The largest 2.5in hard disk drive

The world leader is currently the Toshiba MK3252GSX, which has a storage capacity of 320GB. To achieve this, Toshiba had to use an improved read-write head and boost density with an enhanced magnetic layer.

Heaviest marathon runner

Englishman Lloyd Scott has "run" both the London and New York marathons wearing a 130-lb (59-kg) antique deep-sea diving suit – it took him five days to complete each course.

The world's largest marathon

New York has the largest number of finishers every year, at just under 40,000. Just behind that is Chicago (around 35,000), then London (33,000).

95
the age of the oldest marathon runner

Most marathons run by one person in a year

This record stands at 93, run by American Larry Macon in 2007, while fellow countryman Richard Worsely has run a marathon on 159 consecutive weekends, over courses in the US, Canada, and Mexico.

Four legs good, two legs better

The annual Man vs Horse Marathon has been run in the Welsh town of Llanwrtyd Wells since 1980, and attracts up to 500 humans, 50 equines and a handful of cyclists. Only twice in 27 years has it been won by a runner – Huw Lobb in 2004, in 2h, 5min, 19sec, and Florian Holzinger in 2007, in 2h, 20min, 30sec. The fastest horse has run it in 2h, 2min.

World's fastest marathon course

The marathon course at Chicago, USA, is almost completely flat, and is at sea level, with very few bottlenecks. As a result, more records are set there than anywhere else in the world. New York has one of the slowest courses, thanks to it having a noticeable slope, some very tight spots, and the Brooklyn Bridge. The famous bridge wobbles as the runners go over it, slowing them down.

Marathon kings

Eight of the ten fastest men's marathons have been won by either Ethiopians or Kenyans.

Youngest marathon runner

Budhia Singh – no relation to Fauja – ran his first marathon aged four-and-a-half, in Orissa, India. Budhia finished a 37.5-mile (60-km) race in 6h, 30min.

How long's a marathon?

The marathon is a 26.22-mile race (42.19km), in honor of a soldier in Ancient Greece, who ran about that distance from the town of Marathon to Athens with the news the Persians had been defeated by the Greeks at the Battle of Marathon. The first seven Olympic Marathons (1896–1924) were run over different distances, varying from 24.8 miles (40km) to 26.6 miles (42.8km), depending on the most convenient length in that city. It was agreed that every marathon should be 26.22 miles (40km) in 1924, after the length of what was the most prestigious race in the world, London's Polytechnic Marathon.

Most extreme marathon

The annual North Pole Marathon is the most extreme marathon to be registered with the AIM (Association of International Marathons). It is run over ice in temperatures of between -20 and -30 °C (-4 and -22 °F). It regularly attracts about 50 entrants and in 2008 was won by Korean Byeung Sik Ahn, in a time of 4h, 2min, 37sec. Cathrine Due won the women's title in a time of 5h, 37min, 14sec.

The oldest living marathon runner

This honor goes to Fauja Singh, who completed the 2008 Edinburgh Marathon at the age of 95, and holds the 90+ record for the distance, at 5h, 40min.

Joggling

The record for "joggling" a marathon – that's jogging while juggling three balls – is held by American student Zach Warren, at 2h, 58min, 23sec.

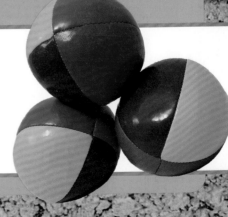

Wiped off the face of the Earth

About 15,000 species are currently nearing extinction. This is partly due to naturally changing habitats but expanding human habitation and deforestation are also to blame. Some scientists believe that about a quarter of all animals and plants may become extinct by 2050 because of climate change.

Dead as a dodo

The dodo is the most famous extinct animal, giving rise to the phrase "dead as a dodo" to describe something undoubtedly, completely, dead. It was a flightless bird that looked like a huge, peculiar duck with a large, hooked bill. It was about 3ft (1m) tall and lived in Mauritius in the Indian Ocean until it became extinct in the late 17th century.

Largest ever deer

The Irish Elk or Giant Deer was the largest deer that ever lived. The latest known remains of the species have been carbon dated to about 5,700BCE. At the shoulders the Giant Deer measured 7ft (2.1m) and

had the largest antlers of any known member of the deer family, measuring 12ft (3.65m) from tip to tip and weighing up to 90lbs (41kg).

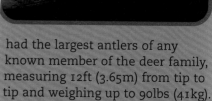

First extinct animal to have its DNA studied

The black-and-white striped zebra is one of the most unusual animals on Earth but it used to have a very close relative called the quagga. Unlike a zebra, the quagga only had stripes on its head and neck. It lived in southern Africa but was hunted to extinction. The last one died in captivity in 1883. It was the first extinct animal ever to have its DNA studied when it was extracted from mounted specimens in 1984.

Bigger than an elephant

The tallest mammoth ever found was 14ft 9in (4.5m) at the shoulder, which is taller than the biggest African elephant. An early relative of the elephant, the mammoths

lived from about 5 million years ago until about 2000BCE. The most famous species is the woolly mammoth, which had a shaggy coat of hair, and huge tusks, which were 16ft (5m) long.

The cat with the dangerous smile

The smilodon had 7in (17cm) long, sharp canines, which were the longest teeth of any of the big cats. Its name means "knife-tooth" and it was known as the saber-tooth tiger. It ate horses, camels, and deer. It became extinct in about 10,000BCE.

Biggest carnivore under threat!

The all-white polar bear is the largest carnivore that lives on land. It often weighs over 1,000lb (453kg) and is 7ft 10in to 8ft 6in (2.4–2.6m) tall. It also has the best sense of smell of all land mammals and can detect a seal from 20 miles away. However, this record-breaking bear is becoming an endangered species because its Arctic sea-ice habitat is melting. There are about 20,000 polar bears but the US Geological Survey predicts the number may drop by two-thirds by 2050.

The largest carnivorous marsupial

Is it a tiger? Is it a wolf? The thylacine is known as both the Tasmanian tiger and the Tasmanian wolf. It was vicious enough to be classed as either. Shaped like a very large dog, it carried its young in a pouch like a kangaroo. The thylacine was the largest carnivorous marsupial of recent times, at up to 6ft (185cm) long. It was common in Tasmania, but was soon being shot by settlers because of the amount of sheep it killed. The last thylacine died in 1936.

Pablo Picasso

According to his mother, Pablo's first word was "piz," an abbreviation of lapiz, which is Spanish for pencil. He received formal training from his artist and museum curator father from a very early age, and is the youngest painter to have exhibited a work, which he did aged eight. By the time Pablo turned 13, his talent had surpassed that of his father, who gave up painting as a result.

Ronnie O'Sullivan

Snooker prodigy Ronnie O'Sullivan scored his first 100 break at the age of 10, his first maximum 147 break aged 15, turned professional at 16, and became the youngest ever winner of a major title – the 1993 UK Championship – when he was 17.

Tiger Woods

The best golfer in the world today could swing a miniature golf club before he could walk, and appeared on a US TV show at the age of two, demonstrating his highly advanced

Freddie Adu

At age 14 in 2004, this American soccer sensation was the youngest-ever professional athlete in the USA. After attracting interest from Manchester United, he now plays for SL Benfica in Portugal after a US record transfer fee of $2 million.

10
age of the youngest Oscar winner

skills with the putter. Tiger was just eight when he won the Junior Golf World Championship and was forced to compete in the 9–10 age group because there wasn't a category for kids as young as him. Tiger Woods is the youngest player to achieve the career Grand Slam, and the youngest and fastest to win 50 tournaments on Tour. He has been voted PGA Player of the Year a record ten times.

Tatum O'Neal

Tatum was the youngest Oscar winner, at just 10 years of age. She received the Academy Award for Best Supporting Actress for her performance in *Paper Moon* in 1973, starring opposite her father, Ryan. In 1974 she received the Globen Globe for New Star of the Year. Tatum went on to star in *Nickelodeon* and *International Velvet* but her star faded as she reached adulthood.

Michelle Wie

The Hawaiian has played golf since she was four, and qualified for the Women's US Amateur Public Links Championship at 10, winning it at 13, in both cases the youngest ever. She shot a round of 64 on a 5,400-yard course at 11, and turned pro at 15. At Stanford, she was unable to play for the golf team as she was a pro, and attended only fall and winter terms. In 2006, she was named in *Time* magazine as "one of 100 people who shape our world." Wie held dual citizenship of Korea and the USA until the age of 20.

Shirley Temple

Shirley is the most famous child actor ever. She began learning to tap dance when she was just three years old, and within two years was starring in Hollywood musicals. She could remember the most complicated routines and was always well prepared. She was so highly thought of when she was seven that a special Academy Award was created for her, the Juvenile Performer Award. The highest grossing star of the American box office during the height of the Depression, she went on to become a United States ambassador.

Ruth Lawrence

From Brighton, England, Ruth Lawrence passed "O" level maths in

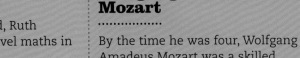

1979 when she was eight, her "A" level Pure Mathematics when she was 10, and got into Oxford University at the tender age of 11. She came first in the Oxford entrance exam, ahead of 529 other candidates. Amazingly, Ruth then graduated after two years instead of the usual three, to become the youngest ever Briton to hold a first-class honors degree and the youngest Oxford graduate.

Wolfgang Amadeus Mozart

By the time he was four, Wolfgang Amadeus Mozart was a skilled clarinet player, and at age five he was able to compose structured

melodies that his father would transcribe for him. Mozart is acknowledged as the most talented child prodigy in classical music and is the only composer in history to have written masterworks in virtually every musical genre of his age. In total Mozart composed an extraordinary 600 works, ranging from chamber pieces to operas.

400
the number of years the longest drought lasted

Melting away

The Arctic ice caps are melting away at an extraordinary rate, shrinking by 20 per cent since 1979, at a rate of 9 per cent per decade. Between April 2002 and February 2009, the Greenland ice sheet shed roughly 385 cubic miles of ice, equivalent to about 0.5mm of global sea-level rise per year. In the Antarctic, over 5,000 sq miles (13,000 sq km) of sea ice has been lost over the last 50 years. Melting Antarctic ice caps are said to have raised the global sea level 2mm a year, that's 15 per cent. Melting ice caps symbolize the effects of global warming on the world climate. Extreme heat waves in 2003 caused more than 20,000 deaths in Europe and more than 1,900 in India and Bangladesh.

Earliest ecologist

The world's earliest ecologist was Greek philosopher Aristotle and his student Theophrastus who, in the fourth century BCE, described the dynamic between animals and their environment. Ecology is a part of biology that deals with the relationship between organisms and their physical surroundings. "Eco" means environment while "logy" denotes a study or science, as in "theology" or "geology."

Under threat

Many of the world's most important heritage sites are being eroded due to pressures of tourism. These include Machu Picchu in Peru, Petra in Jordan and Angkor in Cambodia. At Machu Picchu, landslides on the fragile slopes are threatening whole villages.

Disaster flooding

The world's worst ever flood was in China's Huang He (Yellow) River in 1931, when between 1,000,000 and 3,700,000 died. The river inundated 33,590 sq miles (87,000 sq km), and left 80 million people homeless. The Yangtze and the Huai rivers also added to the toll. That July alone saw seven cyclones, when there are on average two per year. The Huang He is prone to flooding because of the broad expanse of plain that lies around it. This is exacerbated by ice dams, which block the river in Mongolia. The dams, backing up the water, release walls of water when they break.

Most polluted rivers in the world

The Citarum River in West Java, Indonesia, is the world's most polluted river, choked by the sewage of 9 million people and industrial pollutants from hundreds of nearby factories. Scavenging for recyclables has replaced fishing in parts of the river. The Yamuna River in India, another one of the most polluted rivers in the world, is so contaminated that it can hardly maintain any marine life at all. It is at its most polluted where it runs through the city of New Delhi. Here, the inhabitants dump 58 per cent of their waste into the Yamuna.

The world's longest drought

The longest drought in history lasted 400 years – from 1571 until 1971 – and took place in the Atacama Desert of Chile, which is the driest place on Earth. However, in the 18th and 19th centuries, droughts in Cape Verde caused over 100,000 starvation deaths. Drought means a period of time when the water supply in a region decreases significantly. This is usually as a result of a serious lack of rainfall. Drought seriously impacts the agriculture and the ecology of the affected area.

Most polluted city

Of the top 20 polluted cities in the world, 16 are located in China. In Linfen City in the Shanxi Province, which is at the center of China's coal industry, laundry left out turns black before it dries. One-fifth of all humanity live in communities that do not meet World Health Organization standards, with about 2.4 million dying each year as a result of air pollution. Mexico City went from having the world's cleanest air to among the dirtiest in the span of a generation. In 1940, average visibility in the city was 62 miles (100km). Today it is 0.93 miles (1.5km). And in Sukinda, India, which has one of the largest open cast chromite ore mines in the world, 85 per cent of deaths are chromite-related – the drinking water has chromium at levels twice the international standard.

Dribbling in one minute

This world record goes to Jordan Farmar of the Los Angeles Lakers, who bounced a ball 228 times without losing control of it, in February 2008.

Women's world records

The Women's National Basketball Association (WNBA) was formed in 1997 and is the most watched and most lucrative women's professional sports league in the world. It regularly attracts crowds of over 10,000 and features on prime time tv in the US. Star of the WNBA is Lisa Leslie. Now retired, she is a three-times Olympic gold winner (1996–2004); three-time league MVP winner; first player to reach 5,000 career points; and, in 2002, the first woman to dunk a basketball during a game.

Wilt Chamberlain

Wilt The Stilt was 7ft 1in (2.16m) and one of the greatest basketball players in the history of the NBA. In a career that lasted from 1959 to 1974, Wilt set 63 individual NBA records, many of which still stand. These included most points scored in a game: 100; most points scored

in a season: 4029; highest per game average in a season: 50.4; most 50-point games in a season: 45 (no other player has more than 10). Wilt was four times the league's MVP; was selected for 13 All-Star games; and was the winner of two NBA championships.

Highest-earning basketball player in the NBA

This honor goes to Tracy McGrady, whose average annual salary for 2010 is $23 million (£15 million). He plays for the Houston Team. This is a drop from Kevin Garnett, whose wages in the 2009 season were $24.75 million (£16.14 million). For 12 seasons with the Minnesota Timberwolves, Garnett was traded to the Boston Celtics. While these sums may seem like a fortune, golfer Tiger Woods earned over $100 million during the same year.

Joseph Odhiambo

Basketball coach and ball-handling legend Joseph Odhiambo holds the world records for non-stop dribbling of a basketball, at 26h, 40 min. He is also the record-holder for spinning a basketball the longest (4h, 15min); spinning without touching the ball with the other hand (38sec); and simultaneously dribbling the most basketballs for one minute (six).

Mighty Mike

The greatest basketball player off all time is Michael Jordan, whose spectacular career with Chicago Bulls, from 1984–1998, is credited with revitalizing basketball as a spectator sport across the world. He won six championships with the Bulls; five league MVP awards; was in 14 All-Star teams; won two Olympic golds (1984 and 1992); and could stay aloft for so long when he jumped he earned the nickname "Air Jordan". Games sold out whenever he was playing, he shattered previous wage records with salaries in excess of $30 million (£15.5 million), and made even more money from his various product endorsements.

The biggest crowd at an NBA Finals game

A record 41,732 fans watched the Los Angeles Lakers play the Detroit Pistons at the Pontiac Silverdome, Detroit, in June 1988.

Biggest TV audience

The 2007 NBA Finals between San Antonio Spurs and Cleveland Cavaliers were broadcast live in 205 countries in 46 different languages, reaching an estimated audience of 600 million.

The most NBA Championships

The Boston Celtics have won a record 17 NBA Championships while the Los Angeles Lakers have made it to the final the most times at 30. The Lakers have won the Championship on 15 occasions.

Youngest records

Cleveland Cavaliers' LeBron James holds numerous "youngest" records as the youngest Rookie of The Year (2004, aged 19); the youngest to get in the All-Star NBA team (2005, aged 20); to win All-Star MVP (2006, 21 years 55 days); to score 50 points in a game (2005, 56 against Toronto Raptors); and to reach career totals of 1,000, 2,000, 3,000...up to 10,000 points.

South African freedom

Nelson Mandela (b. 1918) is South Africa's first democratically elected leader. Mandela became famous for leading protests against "apartheid" in South Africa, in which black people were denied the same rights as white people. He was wrongfully imprisoned from 1964 to 1990. On his release he helped set up a new multi-racial and fair South Africa. He has received hundreds of awards and was given the Nobel Peace Prize in 1993. Mandela remains a symbol for freedom and equality across the world.

The father of India

Mohandas K. Gandhi (1869–1948) was a political and spiritual leader who led India to her

26
years spent in prison by Nelson Mandela

The original Mr Nobel

Alfred Nobel (1833–96) was the creator of the Nobel Prize. He was a Swedish chemist, engineer, and weapons manufacturer and the inventor of dynamite. Nobel was particularly interested in the study of explosives, and how he could safely manufacture nitroglycerine. In his will he used his considerable wealth to create the now world-famous prize, which since 1901 has honored outstanding achievements in the fields of physics, chemistry, literature, medicine, and peace. The element nobelium was also named after him.

independence from British rule. Trained as a barrister in London, Gandhi was influenced by Hinduism, Christianity, Buddhism, and the authors Tolstoy, and John Ruskin. Gandhi was the first to apply the principle of active non-violent resistance, mobilizing India's masses by his principle of *satyagraha*, "firmness in truth." He was imprisoned several times for his political actions. Called "Mahatma," which means "Great Soul," he was assassinated in New Delhi in 1948, on his way to prayer. Martin Luther King, Jr., said Christ furnished his message while Gandhi furnished his method.

Civil rights in the USA

Martin Luther King, Jr., (1929–68) is the most famous Civil Rights figure in the world and, in 1964, became the youngest ever winner of the Nobel Peace Prize at the age of 35. King was a Baptist minister who became famous throughout the world for his visionary speeches, including his "I have a dream" speech. Martin Luther King, Jr., was murdered at the height of his popularity in 1968.

India's mother of the poor

Mother Teresa (1910–97) was a Roman Catholic nun born Agnes Gonxha Bojaxhiu in Macedonia. In 1971, Pope Paul VI awarded her the first Pope John XXIII Peace Prize. In 1979, she received the Nobel Peace Prize. She taught in a convent school in Calcutta until 1948 when, distressed by the city's poverty, she left the school to dedicate her life to charitable work, helping the poor, orphaned, and sick. At the time of her death her Missionaires of Charity was operating 610 missions in 123 countries.

The first votes for women

Emmeline Pankhurst (1858–1928) led the movement to give women the right to vote in Britain. Prior to her campaign, which became known as the suffragette movement, only wealthy men were allowed to vote. Suffragette protests were often violent and Emmeline went on hunger strike when she was imprisoned. In 1918, her struggles were rewarded when the Representation of the People Act gave women over 30 the right to vote, followed in 1928 by equal voting rights to men.

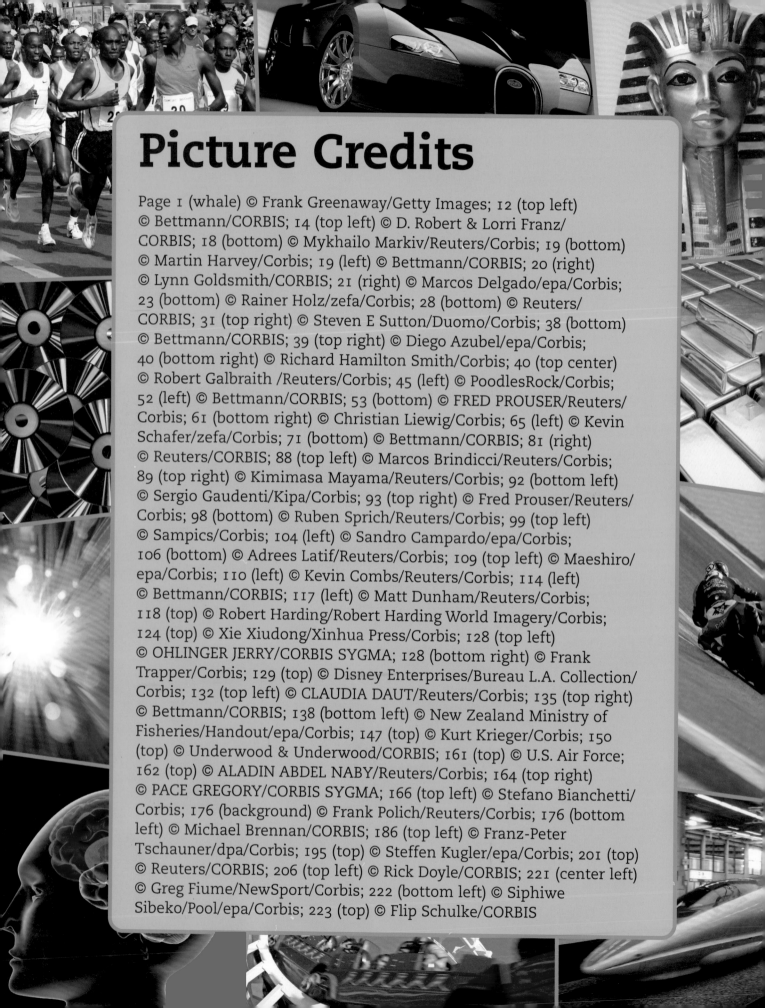

Picture Credits

Page 1 (whale) © Frank Greenaway/Getty Images; 12 (top left) © Bettmann/CORBIS; 14 (top left) © D. Robert & Lorri Franz/CORBIS; 18 (bottom) © Mykhailo Markiv/Reuters/Corbis; 19 (bottom) © Martin Harvey/Corbis; 19 (left) © Bettmann/CORBIS; 20 (right) © Lynn Goldsmith/CORBIS; 21 (right) © Marcos Delgado/epa/Corbis; 23 (bottom) © Rainer Holz/zefa/Corbis; 28 (bottom) © Reuters/CORBIS; 31 (top right) © Steven E Sutton/Duomo/Corbis; 38 (bottom) © Bettmann/CORBIS; 39 (top right) © Diego Azubel/epa/Corbis; 40 (bottom right) © Richard Hamilton Smith/Corbis; 40 (top center) © Robert Galbraith /Reuters/Corbis; 45 (left) © PoodlesRock/Corbis; 52 (left) © Bettmann/CORBIS; 53 (bottom) © FRED PROUSER/Reuters/Corbis; 61 (bottom right) © Christian Liewig/Corbis; 65 (left) © Kevin Schafer/zefa/Corbis; 71 (bottom) © Bettmann/CORBIS; 81 (right) © Reuters/CORBIS; 88 (top left) © Marcos Brindicci/Reuters/Corbis; 89 (top right) © Kimimasa Mayama/Reuters/Corbis; 92 (bottom left) © Sergio Gaudenti/Kipa/Corbis; 93 (top right) © Fred Prouser/Reuters/Corbis; 98 (bottom) © Ruben Sprich/Reuters/Corbis; 99 (top left) © Sampics/Corbis; 104 (left) © Sandro Campardo/epa/Corbis; 106 (bottom) © Adrees Latif/Reuters/Corbis; 109 (top left) © Maeshiro/epa/Corbis; 110 (left) © Kevin Combs/Reuters/Corbis; 114 (left) © Bettmann/CORBIS; 117 (left) © Matt Dunham/Reuters/Corbis; 118 (top) © Robert Harding/Robert Harding World Imagery/Corbis; 124 (top) © Xie Xiudong/Xinhua Press/Corbis; 128 (top left) © OHLINGER JERRY/CORBIS SYGMA; 128 (bottom right) © Frank Trapper/Corbis; 129 (top) © Disney Enterprises/Bureau L.A. Collection/Corbis; 132 (top left) © CLAUDIA DAUT/Reuters/Corbis; 135 (top right) © Bettmann/CORBIS; 138 (bottom left) © New Zealand Ministry of Fisheries/Handout/epa/Corbis; 147 (top) © Kurt Krieger/Corbis; 150 (top) © Underwood & Underwood/CORBIS; 161 (top) © U.S. Air Force; 162 (top) © ALADIN ABDEL NABY/Reuters/Corbis; 164 (top right) © PACE GREGORY/CORBIS SYGMA; 166 (top left) © Stefano Bianchetti/Corbis; 176 (background) © Frank Polich/Reuters/Corbis; 176 (bottom left) © Michael Brennan/CORBIS; 186 (top left) © Franz-Peter Tschauner/dpa/Corbis; 195 (top) © Steffen Kugler/epa/Corbis; 201 (top) © Reuters/CORBIS; 206 (top left) © Rick Doyle/CORBIS; 221 (center left) © Greg Fiume/NewSport/Corbis; 222 (bottom left) © Siphiwe Sibeko/Pool/epa/Corbis; 223 (top) © Flip Schulke/CORBIS